dear Silver

W9-CUZ-852

Palisades.
Pure Romance.

FICTION THAT FEATURES CREDIBLE CHARACTERS AND

ENTERTAINING PLOT LINES, WHILE CONTINUING TO UPHOLD

STRONG CHRISTIAN VALUES. FROM HIGH ADVENTURE

TO TENDER STORIES OF THE HEART, EACH PALISADES

ROMANCE IS AN UNDILUTED STORY OF LOVE,

FROM BEGINNING TO END!

A PALISADES CONTEMPORARY
ROMANCE

dear Silver

LORENA MCCOURTNEY

PALISADES

This is a work of fiction. The characters, incidents, and dialogues are products of the author's imagination and are not to be construed as real. Any resemblance to actual events or persons, living or dead, is entirely coincidental.

DEAR SILVER
published by Palisades
a part of the Questar publishing family

© 1997 by Lorena McCourtney
International Standard Book Number:1-57673-110-3

Cover illustration by C. Michael Dudash
Cover designed by Brenda McGee
Edited by Diane Noble

Printed in the United States of America

Most Scripture quotations are from *The Holy Bible,*
New International Version (NIV)
© 1973, 1984 by International Bible Society,
used by permission of Zondervan Publishing House

ALL RIGHTS RESERVED
No part of this publication may be reproduced, stored in a retrieval system, or transmitted, in any form or by any means—electronic, mechanical, photocopying, recording, or otherwise—without prior written permission.

For information:
QUESTAR PUBLISHERS, INC., PO BOX 1720, SISTERS, OREGON 97759

Again, to my mother.

❧

Bear with each other and forgive whatever grievances
you may have against one another.
Forgive as the Lord forgave you.

Colossians 3:13 (NIV)

One

ilver read the brusque, impersonal letter once, twice, three times, her bewilderment growing with each reading.

Dear Silver:

Although our personal relationship of the past year has been rewarding in many ways, it has become apparent over time that the negative aspects outweigh the positive. Therefore, I believe the decision I've reached to end it at this time is in both our best interests.

I wish you all the best on your new business venture.

Cordially,

Chris Bentley

Silver absentmindedly raked her fingers through the sandy blond tangle of her wild new spiral perm, the corkscrew hairdo her coworker Colleen had enthusiastically endorsed as a "curl with an *attitude*." Her own mental attitude was an even tighter corkscrew as she skimmed the aloof words once more. She undoubtedly would have been devastated by the letter except for one minor point.

Colleen, whose counseling cubicle was near Silver's, dropped a manila folder on the desk while Silver was studying the scrawled signature.

"Here's the Iverson file," Colleen said, then added, "Want to grab a taco for lunch? It's pouring rain, of course, but the water probably isn't more than hip deep." Colleen, a California transplant, was still a bit disgruntled about the amount of rain the Seattle skies could dump in her vicinity.

Silver ignored the facetious weather forecast. She planted her elbows on the desk, chin in her hands, and eyed her dark-haired friend gloomily. "Colleen, how would you characterize my love life?"

Colleen tilted her head warily at this out-of-the-blue question.

"Well?" Silver prodded.

"Give me time. I'm thinking. What brought this on?"

"Just answer the question."

Finally Colleen said, "You have lots of male friends."

"Right. Always the buddy, never the bride. They tell me about the problems in *their* love lives."

"That's because you're a good listener, and you *care*. Look how you helped Jeff and me when things were pretty rocky for us."

"You're avoiding my question," Silver accused. "Maybe because you're remembering how I spent date night of the year, New Year's Eve, baby-sitting the kids in the next-door apartment. Or perhaps you're recalling the 'wonderfully spiritual' blind date whose idea of spiritual turned out to be communing with his broccoli to make certain it didn't object to being eaten."

"Blind dates can be iffy," Colleen murmured.

"Maybe you're thinking about the guy I tried to impress with a fancy flaming dessert, and I set fire to his sleeve? Or the one who made spaghetti for me, and we both wound up with food poisoning?"

To say nothing, Silver added silently to herself, of the man who had *really* broken her heart.

Colleen held up a hand in protest. "Sil, none of that means anything's wrong with your love life. It just means God hasn't sent the right man into your life yet. Twenty-five is not exactly over-the-hill, you know. Didn't you say you'd met an interesting guy while you were out jogging the other day? So maybe things are looking up."

"You think so?" Silver shoved the letter across the desk. "Read this."

Colleen read the frosty good-bye letter. "That's too bad. Breakups are always upsetting. But I don't remember you even mentioning this guy." She sounded mildly accusing.

"Colleen, we both know my love life has always been more like the sinking of the *Titanic* than a Club Med cruise, but this is a new low. Now I'm getting dumped by some guy *I don't even know.*"

Colleen blinked. "What do you mean?"

"I mean I have no idea who Chris Bentley is."

Colleen read the brief letter again. She inspected the envelope, running her finger lightly over the Maraben Inns address. "You're sure? It doesn't seem likely that he'd just pick a name out of the phone book and whip off a Dear John, er, Dear Silver letter."

"I don't know him."

"Both the envelope and the letter are addressed to you." Colleen pointed to the beginning of the letter, which indicated with brisk formality that it was directed to Ms. Silver Sinclair of the Wintergreen Credit Counseling Service, Seattle, Washington. "That's you."

"I can't help that! Colleen, my life is not so overflowing with eligible men that I'd forget the existence of one."

"Then if you don't know him," Colleen inquired with

impeccable logic, "why would he dump you?"

"Maybe it's a trendy new time saving wave of the future," Silver muttered. "Skip the relationship; jump directly to the breakup."

"I can think of a few relationships that might have benefited from that," Colleen agreed. "And in this instance, if you did know this guy, I'd say you were fortunate that the relationship was over. He sounds like Mr. Iceberg of the Year."

Silver straightened in her swivel chair. "Yes, he does, doesn't he? He's had a year's relationship with this woman, whoever she is, yet he's dumping her with no more emotion than if he were canceling a magazine subscription." She snatched the letter out of Colleen's hand. "And listen to this! He's weighed the positive and negative aspects of the relationship, as if it were some mechanical *widget* he's found defective!"

"He even wrote the letter on company letterhead stationery."

"And signed it 'cordially'!"

Cordially! Letters saying your insurance was about to be canceled for nonpayment, or warning that your unpaid bill was about to be turned over to a collection agency, ended with the phony friendliness of *cordially*. Silver knew because she'd received such letters.

"And look—," Silver added, pointing to the initials below the closing, her earlier bewilderment now flaming to indignation—"He even had his secretary type the letter. He must have *dictated* it to her. Can you imagine? This guy has all the sensitivity of a slab of concrete."

She picked up the ringing phone. "Yes?" she snapped, still indignant about the letter. Then she apologized and started over in a more congenial tone. "I'm sorry. Yes?"

"Silver, Karyn Anderson is here," Holly, the receptionist, said. "She doesn't have an appointment. Could you see her after your lunch hour, or should I set up an appointment for later in the week?"

Silver didn't bother to check her calendar. She knew her afternoon was already crammed with appointments. Sometimes it seemed that at any given moment half the population of Seattle was in the midst of a credit crisis. But she knew that Karyn, a young mother caught in a quagmire of financial problems after her husband walked out, wouldn't be here on a lunch hour if some desperate new problem hadn't arisen.

"Just send her in now. I'll skip lunch." Silver looked up to see Colleen smiling knowingly at her. Defensively she said, "What's *that* look all about?"

"What was the subject of Mr. Landeau's most recent office lecture? Something about not getting too emotionally involved with clients' problems? And on whom were his beady little eyes focused during most of that lecture?"

"Look who's talking," Silver scoffed. "Since when did rounding up a crib and baby things for a client become part of the job description of a credit counselor?"

"I'll bring you a milk shake," Colleen said, apparently deciding to detour a self-incriminating discussion of emotional involvement with clients. "And *you* can try to figure out what you did to incur the wrath of one Chris Bentley."

Petite Karyn Anderson, raindrops shimmering in her auburn hair, slipped in as Colleen went out. She indeed had a new and desperate problem. Earlier Silver had worked out a debt-repayment plan acceptable to Karyn's creditors and manageable on her limited salary, but now the parents of her whereabouts-unknown husband were demanding custody of her two children, claiming Karyn was an unfit mother because she wasn't staying home to take care of them. No, Karyn wasn't staying home, Silver fumed; she was out working to pay off the bills their son had run up!

This custody problem was outside the realm of credit counseling, and office rules specifically prohibited giving legal advice, but Silver couldn't simply send Karyn off with that coldhearted information. Instead, she got on the phone to a low-income legal aid service, sweet-talked a lawyer she knew there into seeing Karyn immediately, and wrapped a comforting arm around Karyn's shoulders while the young woman let off emotional steam with a good cry.

Silver watched with a certain frustration as Karyn left the office. Karyn didn't look as discouraged and panicky as when she came in, but how Silver would have liked to offer her the comfort of Christ's love and to pray with her! But she couldn't do that here, of course. More rules and regulations. They were here to solve credit and financial problems, not spiritual ones, as had been pointed out to her before, especially by the new office manager, Mr. Landeau.

Yet so often she could see that a spiritual emptiness was the basis of the real problem. What she would really like to do (an idea that seemed to recur more frequently since Mr. Landeau's arrival) was join or start a Christian counseling service, one that covered all aspects of counseling about personal, marriage, and financial problems from a solid Christian foundation.

But for now, one thing the rules couldn't do was stop her from silently praying for clients on her own time. Which was exactly what she did during the remaining minutes of her lunch hour.

Colleen delivered the milk shake just as Silver was lifting her bowed head, but the thick chocolate shake was melted and watery before Silver had a chance to finish it. She spent the afternoon with a bewildered young couple who had credit-carded themselves into monthly payments almost as large as their income, a single mother trying to cope with a mountain of debt from a child's illness, and an older couple struggling to manage on a small retirement income.

She was too busy to give Chris Bentley and his strange letter more than an occasional passing thought, but at quitting time she realized her subconscious had been gnawing at the subject like a dog with an old bone all afternoon.

Chris Bentley really was a complete and total jerk, she decided. An arrogant, self-centered, coldhearted, insensitive clod. Any woman getting dumped after a year's relationship certainly deserved more than a few impersonal words coldly dictated to a secretary and sent out on company letterhead!

She remembered a letter she'd once received that was *not* a mistake, a letter equally cool and detached. And she remembered how devastated she'd been at Brad's attitude that the relationship that meant so much to her warranted no more than a few casual words of dismissal.

Then she was annoyed with herself. She seldom thought of Brad McAndrews anymore, but this was the second time she'd thought about him just today.

She briskly shoved the letter in her desk and slammed the drawer on it. What had happened with Brad was long ago, and *this* man's insensitivity was none of her business. Tomorrow she'd return the letter with a brief note stating that it had been sent to her by mistake.

She was reaching for her raincoat on the stand by the doorway of her cubicle when another thought struck her. With the letter right here in her office, the woman for whom it was intended obviously had not received it. She retrieved the letter from the drawer and checked the date and postmark. The letter had been written and mailed last Friday. This was already Tuesday, which meant that the other woman had probably spent the weekend, or perhaps even longer, wondering why this important man in her life was ignoring her.

Silver picked up the phone and tapped out the number on the letterhead. She'd use a polite but cool approach in informing Chris Bentley of this peculiar error, so he could get it corrected

15

immediately. The news would undoubtedly be an unpleasant shock to the woman, but *knowing* would be better than being left dangling in ignorance. She might also subtly hint that he could handle the ending of the relationship with a bit more tact and sensitivity than he showed in this letter.

After a dozen empty rings she realized that the business office had no doubt closed at five o'clock. She frowned slightly. The name Maraben Inns sounded vaguely familiar, but she couldn't place it. She flipped to the B section in the bulky Seattle phone book, but apparently Chris Bentley hid behind an unlisted home number.

Nothing to do but wait until tomorrow, then, to call him. The delay frustrated her, and with the frustration came the thought that when she did reach him she might not be so *subtle* about letting him know what she thought of his cold and brittle Dear Silver letter.

Two

The following morning, Silver dialed Chris Bentley's office number during her coffee break. Her opinion of him had not risen after a night of stewing over his arrogant, callous letter.

"Maraben Inns," an upbeat voice said with practiced cheerfulness.

"May I speak to Chris Bentley, please?"

"I'll connect you with his secretary."

A momentary delay and then a more mature voice said, "Mr. Bentley's office."

Silver went along with the formal term and asked to speak to Mr. Bentley.

"May I tell him who's calling?"

Silver hesitated. Given the fact that the letter had to be some strange mix-up, the name *Silver Sinclair* wasn't going to mean anything to Chris Bentley. Yet she didn't want to go into complicated details with the secretary. While Silver hesitated, the secretary repeated the question.

Awkwardly, twisting a long curl around one finger, Silver

reluctantly began an explanation for this call. "My name is Silver Sinclair—"

"Oh, Silver! Just a moment, please. Chris is on the phone, but I'll let him know you're on the line."

Shocked, Silver pulled the phone away from her ear and looked at it, not quite believing what she'd just heard. What did this mean? Why had the secretary reacted as if she knew her?

For the first time a new and unexpected thought tumbled into Silver's mind. Was it possible that only the address on the letter was in error and that *another* Silver Sinclair existed out there somewhere?

After a moment in limbo, the line breathed open. "Silver?" The deep male voice was wary, but the inflection held a definite hint of familiarity.

The widening probability that there really was another Silver Sinclair gave her a disorienting jolt. Logically, two people having the same name wasn't all that unusual. She'd had two Debbie Johnson friends in college. She had never, however, expected to run into an exact duplicate of her own *Silver Sinclair.* It felt eerie, like looking in a mirror and seeing someone else's image.

"Silver?" he repeated into the silence.

"Yes, this is Silver," she finally said as she gathered her scattered wits. "But—"

"You sound a little odd. I hardly recognize your voice."

Of course you don't recognize it. Wrong Silver. She started to explain. "I received your letter, but—"

"I'm sorry, could you hold a minute? We're in the middle of a little problem out at the construction site—"

A click, and she was again in the suspended world of *hold.* She waited, drumming her fingers on the desk, feeling more annoyed every moment. *He dumps a woman, and now he's too busy to give her a minute on the phone.* The wait also gave Silver time to read and reread the curt letter numerous times. Her opinion of it did not improve.

"I'm sorry for the interruption," he apologized when he returned to the line. "You were saying—?"

She hadn't really intended to express her scornful opinion of the letter, but after the frustrating wait she couldn't help herself. "This letter is *so* cold and impersonal. A breakup after two people have been important in each other's lives for a year surely deserves better than this."

"Well, uh—" He paused, apparently astonished at her outburst. "I suppose that's true, because our relationship has been important, but, I, uh—"

Her resentment leaped upward another notch as he floundered under the weight of the admitted fact that he and the other Silver *had* meant something important to each other. Oh, yes, he definitely owed this woman more than that cold, stilted letter!

"Where are you?"

The unexpected question sidetracked her again. *Where?* "I'm here, of course—"

"I just wondered if you were home or here with your Aunt Louise. I drove by the new store when I was passing through Portland a few days ago. It looked busy, and the window display was terrific. I think you're going to do great in that location."

The store must be the "new business venture" referred to in the letter. He sounded sincere, as if he really did care about the success of the store, which rather surprised her.

"Do you have a touch of that bronchitis you had last fall?" he added. "You just don't sound like yourself at all. Have you seen a doctor?"

"I'm fine." She found his concern disconcerting, at odds

19

with the mental picture she had of him as remote and uncaring. Then she realized what was going on here. Thinking she was the other Silver, he, slick as a fast-talking telephone solicitor dangling some phony prize, was trying to detour the conversation away from that incriminating letter. She yanked it back. "About that letter, I just want to tell you—"

"Silver, I'm sorry, I have to take another call. The backhoe hit a water line out at the construction site, and we have water going everywhere. I'll get back to you in a minute—"

Another wait. She granted that a water-line break was undoubtedly a problem, but she couldn't stay on the phone much longer. She had to get back to work.

When he returned, he sounded harried. "I'm going to have to run out there. Look, Silver, perhaps I should have done this in person instead of by letter, but there was Tyler to consider, and I didn't want to cause any unnecessary unpleasantness."

Tyler? Who was Tyler? Okay, it was definitely time to halt this ridiculous little errors-in-identity she'd foolishly stumbled into and set him straight about who she was. "I—"

"But, since you are in town, perhaps we should get together and discuss this after all."

Instantly alarmed, Silver said, "No!"

A shocked silence suggested Chris Bentley was somewhat taken aback by the vehemence of that no. But, of course, he thought this was the other Silver speaking.

"What I mean is—"

He recovered smoothly. "No need to explain. I understand. Well, I think that takes care of everything, then. It's been good talking to you again, Silver. Take care of yourself."

Just like that, he was going to slither out of it! Not a word of apology or explanation or regret to this woman he'd dumped. Silver heard herself beginning to sputter indignantly.

"Are you crying?" he asked, his dismay obvious.

"No, I am definitely not crying! I'm trying to tell you—"

"Silver, I'm sorry, but Mrs. Oliver is signaling that I have another call from the construction site."

"Wait—" She hadn't yet gotten through to him the fact that the wrong woman had his letter, which was the whole point of this call.

"I'll be tied up until late today, but if you decide you want to talk about this, meet me at that espresso and sandwich shop we've been in a few times."

"No, you don't understand—"

"Tommy's, I think it is. Across from that little shopping center near your aunt's house. About nine o'clock tonight."

He hung up before she could say anything more.

Well, she'd certainly bungled *that,* she realized in dismay as she sat there holding the phone with nothing but a dial tone buzzing in her ear. Quickly she dialed again. This time she'd make it quick and to the point, not let herself get sidetracked. He'd no doubt label her *strange* for that muddled first call, but she'd simply ignore that and do it right this time.

But she got a busy signal at Maraben Inns. Then her next client arrived, and she was tied up until noon. By then, when she got through to Chris Bentley's office, the secretary informed her that he'd be out for the remainder of the day.

Now what? she wondered as she sat there tapping her toe in frustration. Wait until tomorrow and try again? Meet him at Tommy's Espresso?

No! Even if that had sounded like a good idea, which it def-initely did not, she was busy this evening. She'd promised to fill in for the woman who usually supervised the nursery during midweek services at church, and she wasn't going to renege on that.

But she would, of course, be through in the nursery before nine o'clock, and it wouldn't be out of her way to go to

21

Tommy's. Of all the espresso shops in Seattle, places she'd never heard of or were miles away, he'd named this one with which she was familiar, conveniently located halfway between church and her apartment.

Okay, she'd do it. She'd pop into the espresso shop at nine o'clock, hand him the letter, offer a brief explanation, and get out. And keep to herself any derogatory opinions of his dumping technique, which wouldn't matter to him anyway.

Later that day she did acquire some interesting information from Colleen, who'd done a bit of research and learned that Maraben Inns was a West Coast motel chain.

"About your Chris Bentley—," Colleen added.

"Not *my* Chris Bentley!"

"Seems he's something of a local celebrity. He won some motel-industry award last year and, before that, Young Businessman of the Year."

"Good for him. Maybe this year he can ask for a raise so he can invest in a personality transplant."

"He doesn't have to ask for a raise. He *owns* the company. All twenty-one motels of it. Twenty-two, if you count the unfinished one under construction out at Bothell. The company also has a reputation as an excellent employer, with generous employee benefits and very low turnover."

Silver refused to let herself be overly impressed even though those facts were rather impressive. She also recalled now that a couple of years ago she'd had a client who worked for a motel chain, perhaps this one, so that explained why the name sounded familiar.

At nine o'clock that evening, however, Silver was not briskly popping in and out of Tommy's Espresso to hand Chris Bentley the letter. She'd forgotten a special choir practice was scheduled after the midweek services this week, which meant she had to keep the nursery open an extra hour. Then Hank Arlands stopped her to discuss some early plans for the children's summer camp the church always held out on one of the San Juan Islands. After that, a guy with whom she had a comfortable "just friends" relationship after a few dates a couple of years ago wanted to talk to her about some complications with a girl he was dating now, and they sat in Silver's car talking for nearly half an hour. It was almost ten o'clock by the time she finally started home.

She slowed her car as she approached the small parking lot of the espresso and sandwich shop. Chris Bentley wouldn't still be there, of course. That abrupt letter and busy pace of his office did not suggest a man inclined to sit around patiently waiting an hour for a woman to show up. Neither was there a vehicle among the motley collection in the parking lot that looked expensive or luxurious enough to belong to an owner of a chain of motels. On sudden impulse Silver braked and turned her secondhand Toyota into the parking lot. A soothing, before-bedtime latte was just what she needed right now.

Inside the espresso shop, the dozen or so customers were all gathered in one jovial group around two tables pushed together. The room was bright and warm, fragrant with the rich scent of coffee and a hint of pastrami. One man was just leaving, going out the side door as she came in the front.

For a moment Silver felt a stirring of alarm. That couldn't be Chris Bentley, still here waiting, could it? She rejected the thought as she watched the man stride to a muddy pickup and pull out a cellular phone, talking on it with one foot braced on the vehicle. He was jacketless, his plaid shirt, jeans, and heavy boots a rough counterpart of the rugged pickup that she was still country girl enough to recognize as four-wheel drive. Definitely not your owner-of-a-chain-of-motels type of vehicle.

She ordered her almond-flavored latte and carried it to a tiny table on the far side of the room, her mind flickering from thoughts of the other Silver to the quick-escape artistry of Chris Bentley to what she should do about the letter now.

Her thoughts were turned inward, her gaze absentminded, and it took at least a minute before the realization of what she was looking at registered on her mind. Her head jerked back. Her eyes blinked.

A jacket. A jacket draped around a chair two tables away, some silky blue material with knit collar and cuffs. And, arced in a half-circle in gold print across the back, a name: Maraben Inns.

Her head swiveled to the direction of the parking lot. That guy making a phone call out there by the muddy pickup *was* Chris Bentley!

She collected more details now. Lanky build, long legs, dark hair sheened to a gleam under the parking-lot lights, an impression of rugged good looks even from a distance. She wasn't the only one watching him, she realized. One of the women from the laughing group was keeping an eye on him with definite interest.

Silver's first reaction was a panicky urge to drop her cup and flee, pushed by a strange feeling that she was already in over her head, but she squashed that ridiculous impulse. She'd wanted to return the letter to him; here he was. She was not going to be intimidated by a handsome face or rugged build. She fumbled in the pocket of her raincoat for the letter.

Still, watching him slam the pickup door and head for the door of the espresso shop with a tight-lipped scowl, an uneasy alarm rippled through her. He was not, she suspected, going to be pleased with this awkward situation.

But this was only going to take a minute, she reminded herself firmly, and it was he, not she, who had made the error with the letter.

Quickly, before she could lose her nerve, she picked up her

cup, wove her way around the next table, and dropped into the empty chair opposite the jacket.

Three

He strode to the table, then glanced around as if wondering if he'd made a mistake, saw his jacket still draped over the chair, and apparently decided she was the one who had made a mistake.

"I'm not looking for company," he stated flatly. He dropped into the chair as if claiming this area was his personal domain and she an unwelcome trespasser.

Up close, she could see the dark curve of his eyelashes, the blue eyes deepening to a ring of midnight around the edges, the angular cut of jaw, even the narrow white line of a scar on his temple. He had a skier's tan, a lighter area around the eyes marking where he'd worn goggles on the slopes. His shoulders filled the plaid shirt with lean muscle, with several inches of solid forearm exposed by a ragged tear in the sleeve. Yet, in spite of the rough clothes, he also had an unmistakable air of self-confidence and authority, a combination that added up to a rugged, no-nonsense sophistication.

Chris Bentley, she decided warily, could hold his own in a corporate boardroom, on a ski slope…and with any calendar of handsome hunks.

Staring at him, it took a moment before the meaning of his words sank into Silver's mind. Then she jerked back indignantly. He thought she was coming on to him! Of all the egotistical nerve! Yet at the same time she had to admit that having some strange woman come on to him probably wasn't all that unusual an occurrence in this good-looking guy's life. And he could probably be as abrupt and cavalier as he wanted in dumping any given woman; others were no doubt already taking a number and standing in line.

She hadn't even noticed a flat package lying on the table until he protectively covered it with one hand.

Okay, get this over with, fast.

"You are Chris Bentley, aren't you?"

His only indication of surprise that she knew him was a slight narrowing of his eyes. The thin scar twitched like a small warning signal with the movement of his heavy eyebrows. He neither affirmed nor denied the identification. "And you are—?"

"We had an appointment. I'm Silver Sinclair. Sorry I'm late—"

His smooth forehead wrinkled into a confused scowl. And confusion, Silver suspected, was not a familiar situation for Chris Bentley. He radiated an aura of high-powered energy and authority under taut, intelligent control. Yet at this moment she'd definitely tilted him off-balance.

"Silver sent you?" he finally asked, apparently deciding that what he thought he'd heard was illogical.

"No. I told you, *I'm* Silver Sinclair." Seeing his confusion took away some of her nervous apprehension, made her feel more in control of the situation. *Let him stew about that for a minute,* she decided with a certain satisfaction.

"I see." He leaned back in his chair, blue eyes speculative as his gaze strolled over her. And as quickly as that her feeling of being in control evaporated.

What did he see as he looked at her? she wondered uneasily as he continued to study her. Because she had gone to church prepared to work in the nursery, where she knew from experience that spit-ups and other accidents were inevitable, she'd worn old leggings and a floppy blue sweatshirt. No lipstick. No perfume, unless it was a faint, lingering scent of baby powder. And her hair? The rebel corkscrews felt as if they were standing straight out from her head.

Not exactly a power outfit.

Unexpectedly, he laughed. "Okay, what is this? Practical joke? That seems a little out of character for Silver, but I suppose she has a right to be annoyed with me."

Silver wished he hadn't done that, laughed. Now *she* felt confused and off balance. The flash of even, white teeth was not unexpected, but the warmth and good humor of the chuckle was. Neither had she expected a small, feminine flutter of reaction.

She corralled an unwanted urge to smile back. This was, after all, the guy who had abruptly ended a year-long relationship with another Silver by sending a cold, business-style letter on company letterhead.

"No, I told you, *my* name is Silver Sinclair."

"Okay, the joke is over," he said impatiently. "What is this? Who are you?" His eyes narrowed with sudden realization. "That was *you* on the phone this morning?"

His suspicious gaze suddenly targeted her as anything from con lady to potential terrorist hiding a bomb in her pocket.

She yanked her wallet out of her purse and flipped it open to her driver's license. He studied the glossy likeness, gaze flicking from the photo to her face and back again.

"So, you see, I *am* Silver Sinclair." She didn't try to keep a certain triumph out of her voice. She pulled the letter from her pocket and threw it on top of the driver's license. "And, as I told you on the phone, I received your letter."

He unfolded the crumpled sheet and read it, a puzzled scowl cutting twin slashes between his dark eyebrows. "Obviously there's been some very peculiar mistake here." For a moment, his earlier hint of confusion returned, but his eyes hardened as his gaze lifted to her face. "But I fail to understand why you tricked me into coming here—"

"Why I did *what?*" Silver gasped indignantly. She had certainly mismanaged the truth a bit when she hadn't instantly corrected his assumption on the phone that she was the other Silver. But tricked him? "You had your important phone call and said meet you here," she finally said. "Then you hung up before I could explain. When I tried to call back, you were out for the day."

He did not appear convinced that he had not been tricked in spite of Silver's explanation, which, she realized with some frustration, had come out sounding both breathless and defensive.

"It wasn't as if I were scheming to meet you," she snapped.

"I also fail to understand your, ah…hostility over this situation. You received a letter meant for someone else. As I said, a very peculiar error, but—" He paused, a split-second bafflement breaking through his own hostile expression before he continued smoothly, "It has nothing to do with you."

"But you did write the letter?"

The direct personal question apparently startled him into saying, "Yes—" before he caught himself and added frostily, "But that really is none of your business, Miss, er, Sinclair."

He spoke her name with a certain reluctance, as if he hated to admit she really was Silver Sinclair.

Silver snatched a deep breath. She had never been a lukewarm person. She did not tend to remain silent about unfairness and injustice. She wrote fiery letters to editors and to advertisers who sponsored TV violence or relied on sexually charged ads to sell everything from heartburn pills to shaving cream. She'd marched in protest against a proposal to tear down a nearby block of wonderful old historic homes and put in a mini-mall; she fought back fiercely when creditors unfairly harassed her clients.

Yet, as he so bluntly pointed out, this private matter really was none of her business. She couldn't tear into some strange man with a criticism of how he handled a breakup with another woman, even if he had been callously insensitive and that woman had the same name as her own.

Even if she knew from personal experience how devastating such a cold, impersonal letter would be to that other woman.

"Now what?" he demanded.

"What do you mean, 'now what?'"

"You're sitting there bristling like a porcupine about to explode, all worked up over nothing—"

Worked up over *nothing?* Her receiving the letter may have been "nothing," merely a peculiar accident, but his writing of the letter was much more than that! And here he was, sitting there all superior, almost laughing at her, and calling her *a porcupine about to explode!*

Okay, he'd asked for it.

She leaned forward, forearms braced on the table, fists clenched. "Yes, I'm worked up! You've acted like an insensitive clod toward this other Silver! First you arbitrarily decide to drop her, apparently without warning or any attempt to work things out. You *dictate* an insultingly impersonal letter to a secretary, complete with the name and address of a formal business style. You—"

"What are you?" he demanded in astonishment. "Captain of the have-a-nice-day police? Issuing tickets to anyone who doesn't meet your standard of cheerful correspondence?"

She ignored the interruption and continued. "You word the letter as if you're dismissing an unsatisfactory employee or returning a defective widget. You close it with a bloodless *cordially*. And then, as a final insult, you send it out on impersonal company letterhead!"

He looked momentarily taken aback by her fiery list and glanced down at the letter lying like a battle line between them. But then he draped both forearms on the table and leaned forward, his nose only inches from hers. "Let me get this straight. You're in this dither just because you don't like the wording or tone or whatever of a letter that wasn't even intended for you?" He sounded as much incredulous as angry. "Just what business do you think it is of yours anyway?"

"Injustice is everyone's business!"

"On the scale of injustices in this world, I think this one ranks fairly low. There are considerably larger offenses to worry about than the flaws…what *you* perceive as flaws," he added with caustic emphasis, "in a private letter ending a relationship."

"Large injustices start as small ones. Maybe if we all tried to be more considerate of each other with the small things in life, they'd never escalate into big injustices—" Silver broke off, suddenly appalled with herself and the way she'd ripped into him and was now lecturing him. Both their voices had risen, and the people in the other group were looking at them curiously.

But he wasn't through yet. "Well, well, a philosopher as well as a literary critic," he mocked.

Okay, she'd gone this far. Why stop now? "You also took the coward's way out by sending a cold-blooded letter instead of facing the other Silver and explaining in person," she added recklessly. "A wimpy—"

That accusation apparently got to him because a hint of insulted outrage, almost a sputter, jumped into his voice.

"You're calling me a *coward* and a *wimp?*"

He looked ready to label her with something even less complimentary, but abruptly he leaned back and laughed again. The heart-strumming flash was the same as before, but the earlier hint of tolerant warmth was lacking. Now he surveyed her almost insolently. "I get it now. You've recently been dumped, haven't you? So now you have it in for the entire male sex. You want to wreak vengeance on *any* man who wants out of a relationship, and I just happened to be an unlucky guy who wandered into your line of fire."

"No!" She stopped short, suddenly aware there could be a pinprick of truth in the accusation. Her breakup with Brad hadn't been recent, but she'd definitely noted similarities between what Chris Bentley had done to the other Silver and what Brad had done to her.

But no way did she hold a jaundiced view of all men! She had a wonderful father, brothers, and cousins; she had good male coworkers; there were terrific men in her church. She wasn't dashing around like some caped avenger in high heels trying to "wreak vengeance" on any stray member of the opposite sex!

He leaped on her small hesitation with rude glee. "So I was right! You have just been dumped."

Silver reached for her wallet, ready to put this encounter to an immediate end, but her shaking hand struck his cup instead. In dismay she watched, as if in slow motion, his cup overturning, spewing coffee like a dark fountain, and Chris Bentley half-rising in his chair. A hot stain spread over his jeans.

"Oh, I'm so sorry!" Silver gasped.

Wordlessly he stalked toward the rest rooms at the rear of the room. Silver heard a giggle from someone in the jovial group. She snatched her wallet out of a puddle of coffee, wiped it across her sweatshirt, dabbed ineffectually at the spilled coffee with a paper napkin…oh, no, there went her latte, too!

With one last, helpless look at the spreading disaster, she turned and fled.

She didn't look back as she dashed to her car and exited the parking lot with a squeal of tires, the only time in her life she'd ever branded rubber on pavement. Once on the street, common sense took over, and she automatically drove carefully, but she felt like a cork about to pop from a bottle until she was safely in the central parking square surrounded by her apartment complex. She turned off the engine and dropped her head between her hands on the steering wheel.

She couldn't remember ever feeling so embarrassed, so ridiculous. Her palms slicked the steering wheel with perspiration, and tears burned her eyes. Her mind replayed the humiliating moments like some rerun with no shutoff switch.

But it was all over now, she assured herself after several minutes of sitting there in the parking lot and resolutely taking deep, steadying breaths. She wiped her eyes with a tissue. What did she care if Chris Bentley thought she was a card-carrying member of the lunatic fringe and a klutz to boot?

She'd never have to see him again.

Four

Chris swabbed a paper towel at the coffee spreading like the map of some dark continent across his jeans.

Who *was* this woman? How had she gotten that letter intended for the real Silver? What possessed her to jump on him like a blond tiger with her complaints and criticisms? And calling him a coward and a wimp!

He still felt uncomfortably damp by the time he tossed the third paper towel in the trash, but he stormed out the men's room door ready to give her a piece of his mind for her busybody interference, her deceptive trick in getting him here, her reckless assault with hot espresso—

He stopped short a half-dozen feet from the table. Empty, the only evidence of her previous presence a soggy paper napkin and a slow drip of coffee over the edge of the table. He just stood there, undecided whether he was relieved she was gone or angry that she'd eluded his wrath.

He suddenly realized people at the other tables were staring at him curiously. Now feeling uncomfortably conspicuous as well as damp, he dropped into the chair and pretended unconcerned nonchalance. He checked his flat parcel, an Etch-A-Sketch he'd picked up for Tyler on his way back from the construction site in Bothell, intending to ask Silver to give it to Tyler for him.

However, since the Silver he'd encountered wasn't the real Silver after all, but some wild-eyed phony—

No, not actually a phony, he granted reluctantly. That driver's license had indeed identified her as Silver Sinclair, with an address near the apartment where he'd lived before he bought the condo in the Magnolia area. And her blue eyes, though stormy enough to warrant hurricane warnings, were actually quite lovely.

He abruptly cut off that irrelevant line of thought. He spotted the letter where it had fallen to the floor and leaned over to retrieve it. The guy operating the espresso machine finally came over with a sponge to wipe up the soggy mess on the table. Chris declined an offer for a replacement of the spilled drink.

He reread the coffee-stained page carefully. The fact that the personal letter was on company letterhead was inexcusable, of course. How in the world had that happened? And the formal business-letter style was equally inappropriate. He'd launch an investigation into all that first thing tomorrow morning, as well as into the incredible error in sending the letter to the wrong woman.

But the letter itself, which this woman had treated as if it were a cockroach crawling out of a drainpipe…was it really all that bad? He was, after all, ending a relationship here, not writing a love letter. Not that he was particularly experienced in either area.

It might be said, he granted reluctantly, that he had, as this fire-breathing critic accused, ended the relationship with Silver somewhat arbitrarily. There had been no quarrels or discussion; he'd simply made the decision and acted on it. That was the way he made decisions; in his position as head of Maraben Inns he couldn't afford to be wishy-washy or indecisive.

But this woman's accusation that he was an insensitive clod! *And* a wimp and a coward. Now that was surely unfair.

He showed the letter to his secretary, Bernice Oliver, as soon as he walked into the office the following morning. As usual, she had arrived early and was already hard at work.

"Do you know anything about this?" he demanded as he thrust the letter at her.

Mrs. Oliver turned from her computer screen to read the letter, which was now beginning to look as if it had taken a detour through the bottom of a birdcage. Her calm, middle-aged face didn't ruffle into awareness of some disastrous error, but she did look puzzled. "No, I don't. Should I?"

"I dictated it as a personal note to Silver, and instead it went out as a formal business letter on company letterhead to some strange woman I don't even know." He pointed to the local address at the Wintergreen Credit Counseling Service.

"I don't understand—"

"I don't, either. But apparently there are *two* Silver Sinclairs in the world—the one I know in Portland and one I don't know here in Seattle—and this letter went to the wrong one."

"I'll check into it immediately." Then, apparently deducing there was more to the situation than a simple isn't-this-odd error, Mrs. Oliver cautiously asked, "Did you have some contact with the wrong Ms. Sinclair?"

Chris had no intention of detailing to his secretary, even though she was friend as well as employee, all that had happened the previous evening, but on impulse he asked, "What do you think of the letter?"

"Think of it?" Her quick gaze scanned the letter again. "It appears grammatically correct, words spelled properly."

"I meant content."

"I suppose I'm…surprised. Silver is such a wonderful and special young woman. When she called the other day—"

"That wasn't her. That was this *other* Silver." The blond tiger Silver.

He paused, unexpectedly struck by all the differences between two women with the same name. The Portland Silver he'd known for a year was petite, dark-haired, with a heart-shaped face and melting brown eyes. She liked to curl up on the sofa with a book, play a leisurely game of chess, create one of her old-fashioned dolls or browse antique stores. This other Silver…tall and slender, but athletic rather than willowy, with a riot of blond hair and a sprinkling of cinnamon freckles. And this Silver, Chris suspected, seemed more inclined to throw a book than read it.

"This is all very confusing." Mrs. Oliver gave him a small frown, as if the complicating existence of two Silver Sinclairs were somehow his fault. "You did write the letter?"

"For personal reasons, I recently came to the conclusion that it would be best to terminate my relationship with Silver. I composed this letter. The Silver Sinclair who received it took strong exception to the tone and wording. She, in fact, called me an insensitive clod." He was almost certain Mrs. Oliver's lips twitched as if she were trying to keep from laughing at that point, but she returned his suspicious gaze with bland inno-cence. "That's why I'd like your opinion on the letter."

Mrs. Oliver studied the page carefully. As usual, when her opinion was consulted, she gave it bluntly. "It sounds like something a lawyer might write if he were concerned about a potential lawsuit for breaking a contract."

"I don't think it's *that* bad," Chris protested.

Mrs. Oliver removed her glasses and tapped her lower lip with the earpiece as she studied him. "I presumed you were going to ask Silver to marry you one of these days."

"I thought about it for a time, but then I decided it wouldn't be the right thing to do."

"I suspect she's also expecting a marriage proposal. So it might have been more considerate, if you felt you *must* break off with her, to use language that made your relationship sound like something more personal than an unsatisfactory business deal."

Mrs. Oliver's critical opinion, much too close to what he'd heard in a more fiery version last night, was not what he wanted to hear. He abruptly dropped discussion of the merits of the letter.

He nodded curtly. "Just find out how this happened, as well as who's responsible."

"Yes, Mr. Bentley, I'll do that immediately."

Mrs. Oliver never used that formal "Mr. Bentley" with him unless he'd done something to warrant her disapproval. He didn't have to ask what it was this time. Mrs. Oliver liked and approved of Silver; she *didn't* approve of his dropping her.

"Oh, Mr. Bentley," Mrs. Oliver called after him as he strode toward the door to his private office, "do you want the letter to go out again, this time to the correct Silver Sinclair?" Her words were business-office polite, but her icy tone relegated this deed to the level of sending a poison-pen letter to a favorite aunt.

"I haven't decided yet," Chris muttered. "Just put it on hold for now while I think about it."

He didn't, however, have much time to consider it that morning. The small crisis of the water-line break was over, but the phone call from his lawyer on an interesting new subject came only minutes after he'd settled at his desk with a mound of paperwork. He flicked the speakerphone switch so he could keep his hands free while talking, red pencil checking and underlining items about costs at the construction site even as he carried on the conversation.

"You're right about the Golden Lighthouse," said Dick Richardson, referring to the motel chain about which Chris had instructed him to make inquiries. "There are definitely problems in the company since the owner's death several months ago."

Through an acquaintance, Chris had accidentally discovered that considerable infighting was going on among the heirs of the chain. He'd immediately caught the scent of opportunity, a kind of sixth sense that had served him well in the past. He wouldn't have acquired the choice location out in the rapidly growing little town of Bothell if it were not for that scent sensitivity.

"Are they planning to sell?"

"From what I've been able to uncover, several of the heirs would like to sell. Another heir, a grandson, wants to take over, but he hasn't got the money to buy the others out. His mother is trying to strong-arm everyone into financing him, but some of the other heirs think he's an irresponsible flake and couldn't run a lemonade stand, much less a chain of motels. I get the impression there are also other, ongoing undercurrents of family hostility. In any case, it's turning into a rather messy family feud."

"You'd think, as shrewd as the old man was in building up the chain, that he would have arranged his affairs to prevent squabbling."

"You'd think so, but apparently he didn't. Could you swing this, Chris, if they do want to sell? It's going to take big money." Dick didn't sound doubtful; it was merely a professional question.

Chris hesitated. He was already deep in debt, of course, and he'd have to restructure his entire debt load to launch this. But what dynamic, growing business wasn't seriously in debt? If he could swing this, it would almost double the size of his operation without the inevitable complications and delays associated with new construction.

If he made a wrong decision here and got in over his head, he could risk losing everything he'd worked so hard to accumulate. Still, he hadn't gotten where he was by being afraid to leap for the stars…without a parachute. And he wasn't going to climb even higher if he stopped leaping now.

What would Ben think? Ben wouldn't think he could do it, of course. In the past, even when he had pulled off something impressive, his grandfather had attributed the success to blind luck, not financial and business competence. But maybe *this* time he'd see things differently.

"I'll figure a way to manage it," he assured Dick now. "Do you know who's handling the legal situation for the family?"

"At this point I think everyone has his own lawyer."

"A whole rattlesnake den of them, eh? Exactly the kind of situation you lawyer guys love, a little business for everybody so you can all afford your BMWs," Chris teased.

His old friend Dick was not insulted. "We don't make the rules," he said cheerfully. "We just look for the loopholes. And just because you prefer that hopped-up motorcycle you roar around on, don't be so high-and-mighty about those of us who prefer our transportation with a bit more creature comfort."

The two men laughed comfortably together.

"You want me to put out feelers about buying the chain, then?"

"Yes, and I'd also like to know, if the chain isn't immediately available, if one or more heirs might sell their shares individually."

"I assume it's set up so they can't do that. But, if it's possible, it would certainly give you an inside position from which to pounce on the other shares." Dick sounded admiring of the shrewd move, although, after a moment's thought, he added skeptically, "Or you might simply find yourself hopelessly entangled in the family squabbles."

Chris laughed. "Spoken like a true lawyer. Just check it out for me, okay?"

"Will do."

When the conversation ended, Chris glanced toward the wall on his left at the framed photo of the single modest motel with which he had begun Maraben Inns, named by joining his grandparents' names, Mara and Ben. The soaring possibilities and raw challenge of this new situation sent spikes of adrenaline charging through him. *I can do it, Ben. Just watch me!*

He kept a lunch date with the contractor handling construction at the Bothell site, bluntly pinpointing the unsatisfactory items he'd discovered after spending the previous afternoon on the muddy grounds, crawling into spaces he knew he wasn't expected to inspect.

Mrs. Oliver followed him into his office when he returned. She kept her hands clasped, forefingers steepled, as she explained what she'd discovered about how the letter got delivered to the wrong Silver Sinclair.

"So it was, in a roundabout way, my fault after all, and I can only say I'm sorry," she concluded. "I'm sure my niece meant well."

Chris dismissed the odd incident with a wave of his hand. "The whole thing is nothing more than the proverbial tempest in a teapot. No harm done." What did he care that some strange, fiery woman had a derogatory opinion of how he'd ended a relationship?

An unexpected thought occurred to him: Would she feel differently if she knew the odd details of the mistake? He *could* give her a call....No. Ridiculous. What difference did it make if she thought he was an insensitive clod and a wimp?

His fingers drummed the teak desk. Because, inexplicable as

it seemed, he *did* care what she thought.

Mrs. Oliver repeated her earlier inquiry. "Do you want the letter to go out again, to the correct party?"

"I still haven't decided."

"I'll just leave the original here on your desk, then." Mrs. Oliver discreetly tucked the battered letter under a bronze paperweight in the shape of the Space Needle. "Again, I am sorry. If you'd like, I can call the local Silver and explain and apologize—?"

"No, don't bother. It's no big deal."

He kept reminding himself of that all afternoon, trying to toss Seattle Silver's opinion aside as irrelevant. But it nagged at him like a poison-oak itch. *Insensitive clod. Wimp.*

Chris had dinner with the manager of one of his southern California motels, who was in town to discuss a possible expansion project, and then he went home with a loaded brief-case of work. He spread papers in a semicircle around a cup of coffee on the old pine dining table and settled down to study some revised cost figures for the Bothell construction site.

Yet the first thing he picked up was the letter, which had somehow found its way into his briefcase. He frowned at the piece of paper that was beginning to feel like a wart he'd once had, something ugly that wouldn't go away. With sudden exasperation he crunched the letter into a ball and tossed it toward a nearby plastic wastepaper basket. He missed the easy shot, and the crumpled ball lay on the silver gray carpet like an oversized, accusing eye, glaring printed words at him.

Reluctantly, he retrieved the crumpled ball and read the all-too-familiar words once more.

If he took a completely objective view, he acknowledged grudgingly, the words could perhaps be viewed as a bit colder and more impersonal than necessary. He might have chosen something less frigid than that phrase about weighing the positive and negative aspects of the relationship. And *cordially*—

"Okay, admit it," he muttered to himself, crunching the page again. The letter wasn't just a *bit* cold and impersonal; it was a disaster. Pompous and aloof, worded with all the sensitivity of a wrecking ball smashing into a building. Silver would have been bewildered and devastated if she'd received it.

Perhaps any letter was a mistake; the fact that this one went astray offered him a second-chance opportunity not to make the break with Silver at all.

The phone rang, his unlisted private number, and he reached for the cordless instrument lying on the far side of the table. He felt a spark of uneasiness before he picked it up. What if it was Silver, Portland Silver? What would he say to her? But it was his brother's cheerful, teasing voice that greeted him.

"Hey, Big Brother, how's the Mighty Motel Mogul?"

Chris laughed, glad for the interruption, glad, as always, to hear from his brother. "I'm fine. Hard at work mogul-ing."

"Pile of work spread on the table? Lunch and dinner business meetings scheduled from now till your old age? Church squeezed into an hour on Sunday? No social life? C'mon, Chris," Brian scolded after painting the details of Chris's life all too accurately. "You gotta get a life. At this rate all you're going to get is ulcers."

"Big brothers give advice to little brothers, not the other way around," Chris scolded with mock severity. Although, with shoulders like a fullback, two inches in height on his older brother, and a faith large enough to take him to a tiny church on some remote, windswept prairie in Montana, Brian was no longer "little brother" in anything except years. "If all you called for was to tell me to eat my vegetables—"

"No, I called because I've got big news. Are you ready for

this? You're going to be an uncle! Carol and I are expecting a baby in September."

"Hey, that's terrific! Congratulations. Are you going to have one of those tests—sonograms, aren't they?—that tells you if it's a boy or girl?"

"What do you know about sonograms and pregnancy?" Brian sounded astonished.

"Big brothers know everything." Actually, all he knew about it was that some friend of Silver's had had such a test done a few months ago, and he'd been amazed that such a thing was possible. And also, he had to admit, a bit envious. Wouldn't it be a thrill to see such a miracle of your own in progress?

"We considered it," Brian said, "but we decided we'll just let God surprise us. Right now we're arguing about names."

"Do I get a vote?"

"If you'd get your nose out of the motel business for a minute, you could get married and have one of your own to name."

Chris ignored that friendly jibe. "Okay, so I won't ask for a vote. But look, Brian, if you could use some extra money—I mean, I know having a baby is expensive."

Brian had never told Chris what he earned as pastor of the small, rural church, but Chris knew it couldn't be much. Not that he thought Brian should have done anything other than follow his heart into the ministry; he just wanted to help out if there was a need. He'd long ago offered Brian a full share in the company and its profits, but Brian had turned it down.

"We're fine. The Lord's looking after us. A rancher brought us two hundred pounds of potatoes a while back. We're having fried potatoes, mashed potatoes, baked potatoes, scalloped potatoes. Tonight it's something Carol is calling Potato Surprise."

Chris laughed. Their parents would be so proud of Brian if

they could see him now! He was tempted to repeat his offer of financial help, but he knew Brian would simply refuse, so all he said was, "Carol's a great woman, Brian. Take good care of her."

"I plan to." Brian paused, then asked tentatively, "Chris, is everything okay?"

"Sure, everything's great. I'm looking into the possibility of a big expansion project. Why do you ask?"

"Sometimes you just sound a little...hollow."

"Are you going to get up on your pulpit now?" Chris teased.

"Yes, I am," Brian announced. "There's nothing lacking in your faith, Chris. I've seen that in all you did for me and in how you stood firm against Ben's scorn and pressure all those years. I know how generously you contribute to the church and other worthy Christian causes. But sometimes I'm concerned about your...priorities."

"You don't see my name on any Fortune 500 list, do you?" Chris said lightly.

"Is that your goal in life?"

Chris detoured that question. "At the moment my goal is just to acquire this other chain of motels. My Bible and I are not strangers," he added, the words coming out more defensive than he intended.

"Good. I'm glad to hear it." Brian hesitated, as if he were considering saying something more on this subject, but finally all he said was, "You eat those vegetables, hear?"

"I'll do that."

Chris put the phone down and went back to his paperwork. Even when Brian got after him, talking to his "baby" brother always lifted Chris's spirits. But a few minutes later, uncharacteristically unable to keep his mind on insulation and plumbing and heating figures, he tossed down his pen and rubbed his eyes. He was delighted with his brother's good news. He was excited about the possibility of acquiring the Golden

Lighthouse chain. Yet, inexplicably, he also had this odd restless feeling, maybe even hollow, as Brian had put it.

He got up and walked to the far side of the huge living room, where a wall of glass looked south to Elliott Bay and a magnificent display of glittering city lights. The Space Needle rose against the skyline like some exotic night-blooming flower, and points of light dotted the dark waters of the bay like captured stars. He opened a window, letting the cold night air coming in over the waters of Puget Sound flow over him.

It was a spectacular view, one of the reasons he'd bought the condo, although he was usually too preoccupied even to notice the changing colors of the water or the myriad lights. He turned and surveyed the interior of the condo, seeing it with a critical clarity that usually escaped him.

The living room was sparsely furnished, lonely islands of furniture huddled together as if fearful of the empty space surrounding them. In the dining room, the oak chairs and pine table, which had come from his old apartment, didn't match. He'd ordered the sofa and love seat for the living room sight unseen from a furniture store, impatiently telling the clerk, when she asked about color, just to bring him something that wouldn't clash with anything. The result was a muddy neutral that Silver, Portland Silver, had laughingly named floodwater tan. The lamps and end and coffee tables he'd conveniently bought from the couple moving out of a neighboring condo, never paying attention to the fact that he hated the ornate fussiness of ruffled shades and dark panels carved with a design that looked like snakes peering through writhing vines. The only thing he really liked was the soothing silver gray carpet. And that had been here when he bought the place.

He'd kept thinking he'd get around to getting some appropriate furniture or hiring a decorator to come in and do it all up right, but somehow he'd just never found the time. When he had people to entertain, he just took them out.

Now, something meaningful lurked in his awareness of the fact that he had no time to improve the interior setting of his home or even notice the spectacular exterior view, but he impatiently brushed it aside before it could jell into full-blown disquiet. Was he feeling this way, all restless and vaguely dissatisfied, because of the decision he'd made to break up with Silver?

He was fond of her. She was a wonderful woman, a terrific mother to Tyler, and little Tyler himself was everything a man could want in a son. And yet something was missing.

He sighed. *Guidance, Lord, I need guidance.*

And maybe, he thought ruefully as he eyed the crumpled letter again, *some lessons in how not to be an insensitive clod.*

Five

ilver forced the entire episode with Chris Bentley and the letter out of her mind. It hadn't been one of her finer moments, true, but it was no earth-shattering disaster. It was even possible that the odd situation might have positive results. Compared to her, the other Silver Sinclair would surely look wonderfully sweet and normal. Maybe Chris Bentley would rush back to her, eternally grateful that the letter had gone astray, and sink on bended knee to propose.

She spent Thursday evening on a women's crisis hot line, where she volunteered a couple times a month. On Friday evening she worked out at her health club, ending with a fast-action game of racquetball with a friend. She turned down a Saturday night date with the guy she'd met jogging a couple weeks ago. No, she wasn't down on men in general, as Chris Bentley had jeered. But this guy, with his invitation to "have a couple of beers," was definitely not one she wanted to spend even an evening with, let alone a lifetime.

On Saturday morning she made her weekly call to her parents in Idaho, cleaned the apartment, and did a load of wash.

After lunch she rewarded herself with an exhilarating bike ride. The winter day was gray and misty, but she caught occasional glimpses of the Space Needle as she pedaled and coasted over the hills of Seattle.

The mist had advanced to a steady drizzle, headlights were coming on, and her shoulders and pant legs were soggy by the time she returned home. She felt both tired and invigorated, ready for a hot bath and a lazy evening. She chained her bike to the rack and started up the outside stairs to the balcony walkway fronting the second-floor apartments, bicycle helmet swinging jauntily from her fingers.

A male figure was standing on the balcony walkway several doors down, thumb planted on the buzzer beside a door. Her door, she realized in surprise as she strode forward. A tall man, ruggedly built, dark-haired, in jeans, heavy boots, and a brown leather bomber jacket....

No, surely not!

Yes.

There he stood, in the flesh. The last person she had ever expected to see again, certainly one of the last she ever *wanted* to see again. Her first inclination was to turn and run before he spotted her.

Too late.

Chris Bentley eyed the swinging bicycle helmet warily. "You're not planning to clobber me with that, are you?"

One little accident with a cup of hot espresso, and he acts as if she's a major menace to society!

Silver ignored the question and, narrowing her eyes, countered with one of her own. "What are you doing here? How did you get my home address?" Her last name and initial were in the telephone book, but discreetly, without an address.

"It was on your driver's license."

"And you remembered it just from that?" His powers of observation impressed her even as she chastised herself for the foolish melodrama of whipping out her wallet to show him her name on the license.

"I once had an apartment not far from here," he said as he eyed the sandy blond cyclone that not even dampness and several hours under a bicycle helmet could intimidate. "Your hair is different from the photo. Very nice," he added.

The unexpected compliment rattled her, but she hid the feeling under a sharp retort. "I assume you didn't come here just to discuss my hair."

Just then he reached for her arm, lightly nudging her toward her apartment door. She reacted to the unexpected touch by flinging her own arm upward to shove his aside, whacking him in the jaw with the swinging bicycle helmet in the process. And then, feeling a little foolish, she realized he was merely trying to make space for a couple to pass by them on the narrow walkway.

"Sorry," she muttered after the couple squeezed by. Chris opened and closed his mouth while rubbing his jaw. Silver suspected he was exaggerating the effects of her unfortunate blow but reluctantly asked, "Did I damage anything?"

Instead of answering, he shrugged, then asked, "Tell me, do your dates usually wear full body and face protection? A little something from the CIA or NASA perhaps, to ward off blows and scalds?"

"You're not a date," Silver pointed out. "And you still haven't told me why you're here."

Another interruption came in the form of the elderly man for whom Silver occasionally did grocery shopping when his arthritis was acting up. "Feeling better today?" she asked, as he limped by with the support of his cane.

"Not quite ready to take you dancing, but maybe one of these days," he responded with a wink and a grin.

They laughed together at this ongoing joke between them. But Silver's amusement ended abruptly when she returned her attention to Chris. "Now, to get back to why—"

He interrupted with a grin. "Why my thumb was glued to your doorbell?"

He'd taken the words from her mouth. Silver merely nodded, momentarily speechless.

His tone softened. "First, I'm here because I want to apologize. It was one of those days when everything went wrong, but that's no excuse for some of the things I said the other evening, and I am sorry."

The apology surprised her, and Silver felt a twinge of sympathy in spite of her earlier skepticism. She was not unfamiliar with frustrating days that left her feeling as if she could sharpen pencils with her teeth. "Did you fix your problem with the broken water line?"

"No serious damage, but it did make a mess."

"I noticed at Tommy's that you'd torn your shirt."

"I caught it on something while I was crawling around under the new motel. Which was right after I bumped my head on a concrete ledge. Which was after I discovered some expensive mistakes in the heating system. Then, when I was ready to leave, I found a flat tire on the pickup, had to get down in the mud to change it, and then discovered the spare was also flat. But none of that is any excuse for my uncalled-for remarks."

"I didn't expect you to be there still. I was an hour late."

"I was also worried about Silver. The other Silver," he added after a pause, as if he were still having trouble with the two-Silvers situation. "I was sure she'd meet me to talk things over, and she's always very punctual. When she didn't show up, I was worried she'd had an accident or something."

"It didn't occur to me you'd worry," Silver admitted. "I'm sorry about that. I'm also sorry about spilling the coffee on you. I hope you weren't burned."

"Actually, your comments were considerably more scalding than the coffee," he said with a wry smile.

"I also may have been a bit...harsh in my judgment," she conceded. "Which, as you pointed out, was none of my business anyway. So I apologize for that." She dug in her jacket pocket for her door key.

Another tenant, a woman carrying a baby in a harness on her back, wove between them on the walkway. A few steps behind her were the newlyweds who had just moved in, holding hands as usual.

Chris suddenly leaned against the railing, hands braced on the black wrought iron, lean legs crossed at the ankles. His gaze was speculative, as if he had all the time in the world.

Silver pointedly pushed back her jacket sleeve and looked at her watch. The cold evening air was beginning to seep through her wet pant legs, and a frigid trickle of collected rain had started down her back.

But Chris didn't seem to notice her impatience to go inside. "Another reason for my coming here," he began, "was that I thought you might be interested in an explanation. About the letter, I mean." He smiled, as if somehow knowing she'd be unable to reject that tempting offer.

"I might be," she agreed, reluctant to sound as curious as she was.

"It wouldn't have happened except for several coincidences at the office. To begin with, I have a secretary who has been with me for years, a wonderful woman and a good friend. And a great secretary, very competent and efficient."

"I assume there's a *but* in there somewhere?"

"Mrs. Oliver is a widow, without children of her own. But

she has this enormous family of brothers and sisters and nieces and nephews and cousins and second cousins, and on and on. She's the mother hen of the clan and is always finding places for them to live or work, or counseling them through their romances. She's one who lives her faith."

"What do you mean?"

He paused to let a couple of children Silver occasionally baby-sat dash by. "She loves her Lord with all her heart…and loves her family with the same all-encompassing love that she knows God has for her."

Chris's mention of God's love surprised her, but she remained silent as he went on.

"Anyway," he continued, "a week ago Friday Mrs. Oliver came down ill, so she called a niece to come in and substitute at the office for her. Also hoping, I suspect, that we'd be so impressed with Melissa that we'd find a full-time job for her. It's worked before. We must have a half-dozen of the clan on the payroll."

"So you're blaming the letter on niece Melissa?" Silver challenged. "You're telling me she just blithely waltzed into your office—"

Again, Chris seemed to read Silver's thoughts and interrupted. "And decided this was a good day to write the other Silver a good-bye letter, and she then extracted your address out of thin air?" He shook his head slowly. "Is that what you were going to say?"

Again, Silver found herself speechless. She nodded mutely.

Chris scowled. "I learned Thursday evening that I had to go out of town on an unexpected weekend business trip Friday morning, so I worked late dictating a number of letters. I left the tapes for Mrs. Oliver to transcribe the next day. However, since she was ill, it was her niece Melissa who transcribed the letters. Mrs. Oliver would have known the letter I'd dictated to

Silver Sinclair was personal, to be typed in that style, on my personal stationery, not the company letterhead. She handles many personal matters for me—"

"Birthday and Christmas gifts. Sympathy and get-well cards. Flowers when appropriate."

"She has excellent taste," he said defensively at her obvious scorn. "And I trust her judgment. People often compliment my gifts and cards."

"Which says marvelous things for *her* taste and sensitivity, if not necessarily for yours," Silver murmured. "But, if she is such a marvel of competence, I don't understand how I became involved."

Patiently he continued with the peculiar odyssey of the letter. "Mrs. Oliver keeps in her desk, rather than on the company computer, a list of a few names and addresses for my personal correspondence. But Melissa didn't know that, and so, since my dictated letter to Silver Sinclair didn't give an address, she searched the computer files for one. She found the name under a listing of resource people, apparently figured you had to be the right person—after all, how many Silver Sinclairs could there be in the world?—signed the letter in my absence, and mailed it off." He paused reflectively. "I don't know how you got on that list."

"A couple of years ago I had a client at the credit-counseling office who worked for a motel chain. It was probably your company. I suppose I was on the list of resource people as a potential source of assistance for other employees with credit and financial problems."

"Sounds plausible."

The story, Silver reflected, made a certain weird sense. Yet a point of logic was missing. She shook her head. "I don't see how any secretary, even a temporary one, could fail to recognize that this was not your standard business letter and should be handled differently. Surely your Mrs. Oliver wouldn't send in someone totally incompetent and irresponsible, even if she was a niece?"

"I think Mrs. Oliver had every reason to believe her niece would be a satisfactory substitute. Melissa has held other secretarial jobs. Mrs. Oliver also didn't know that I wouldn't be in the office that day. But it turns out there was another complicating coincidence."

"Which was?"

"It seems that, unknown to Mrs. Oliver, her niece recently found a new goal in life. She wants to be a rock star. She sings with a group called Exploding Galaxy under the name Starr. I understand they appear in black leather draped with chains of paper clips. Barefoot."

Rock, particularly of the black-leather-and-barefoot variety, was not Silver's choice in music, but she knew some of the local names. "I'm afraid I've never heard of them."

"Not surprising, considering that their audience usually consists of some outraged neighbors who object to their practice sessions. But on Friday, fortunately or unfortunately, depending on your point of view, I suppose, Melissa got a call at the office telling her that Exploding Galaxy had just been hired for a Saturday night gig out at Snohomish because another band had backed out. At that point Melissa's mind apparently went into orbit, because it certainly wasn't on her work. I doubt the contents of that letter even penetrated her brain as she was whipping it off to you. Mrs. Oliver, by the way, sends her regrets and apologies about the mix-up."

Chris seemed to sense Silver's skepticism and quickly added, "Melissa also, rather than sending in a subscription order for a local magazine I wanted, managed to sign me up for a diaper-delivery service. Figure that one out. And tell me how to stop a very determined diaper service from delivering two dozen diapers to my office daily."

The image of Chris Bentley snowed under in a blizzard of diapers was enough to make Silver giggle in spite of a determination to remain cool and aloof. She couldn't quite cut off the laughter, but she did suggest, "They might double as oversized handkerchiefs. You could enclose one with every Dear Silver letter you send out for the recipient's tears."

"Mrs. Oliver says they're wonderful for dusting. Or we could fly them from all the company vehicles as symbols to advertise the fact that children are welcome at Maraben Inns."

"You might redecorate your office with them. Start a trendy new diaper decor."

Unexpectedly, they grinned at each other in companionable silliness, and Silver felt a not unpleasant little shiver of reaction. But out of the convoluted story he'd just told her leaped an incriminating bit of information that wasn't so amusing.

"Even if niece Melissa made some rather monumental errors in judgment, the fact remains," she pointed out, "that *you* composed the letter in all its glorious, coldhearted insensitivity."

"You said you may have been a bit harsh in your criticism of it—"

"I still don't think you did right by this other Silver," Silver argued stubbornly. "Especially considering the intimacy of a year long relationship."

Silver broke off as Chris's easy grin vanished. He straightened at the railing, long legs uncrossing. "If you're using *intimacy* with the usual meaning, you're quite mistaken," he said stiffly.

Silver flushed, embarrassed at having jumped to a conclusion that was none of her business. That it was a wrong conclusion, and one that obviously did not sit well with Chris Bentley, surprised her, however, given the pathway of so many current relationships.

"Actually, I've given your criticism of the letter considerable thought and finally decided you were right." He made the statement with a certain defiance. "I came to ask if you'd be willing to help me write something more appropriate."

Silver took a step closer to peer up at him in astonishment. "You want me to help you write a letter dumping this other Silver?"

"That's a rather blunt way of putting it. Even I, insensitive clod that I am—" He dipped his dark head and rugged shoulders in a mocking bow—"Even I prefer to think of it as terminating a relationship rather than 'dumping.'"

"Why me?"

"When I have a problem, I always look to the top expert in the field for assistance." His smile was so blandly innocent that Silver couldn't tell if he was offering a compliment or taking a sly dig at her.

"Surely you've had a fair amount of experience at relationship termination." She eyed his rangy build, dark hair, and expressive blue eyes, the intriguing mystery of that thin scar on his temple. He even gave the impression that he could be quite charming if he chose. Oh, yes, he was much too attractive not to have dumped his share of women. "You don't look like hermit material to me."

"Actually, this is the first relationship in which I've felt sufficiently involved that I thought an…official ending was necessary. If I were the busy Don Juan you seem to think I am, dumping women right and left, don't you think I'd be a little better at it than I am?"

He lost patience while she reflected on that. "I really don't care what you believe, but it's true. My work has never left me with much time for relationships of any continuity or depth."

Okay, maybe she was being one-sided, Silver admitted grudgingly. In person, he didn't come off nearly as aloof and coldhearted as he had in that letter. "So how do you usually handle breakups?"

"I've never really considered them breakups. There simply wasn't that much to any of the other relationships. My work has always been more important. I'd just stop calling, and have Mrs. Oliver or my answering machine screen out calls I didn't want to receive."

"How wonderfully sensitive," Silver murmured.

He stared at her, jaw visibly clenched as he restrained his temper. "Okay, we've already established that I'm what might be called 'sensitivity challenged,'" he finally growled. "But I'm willing to learn. Do you want to help me or not?"

Six

He threw the words out less as invitation or plea than as challenge. Silver's first inclination was to hurl back, *I'm a credit counselor, not a miracle worker!*

But the surfacing of a basically more caring and generous aspect of her nature—and perhaps, she had to admit guiltily, curiosity—overruled that inclination. So instead she said, "Why do you want to break up with the other Silver?"

"I have no intention of spilling all the personal details."

"Perhaps because you don't come off looking too good?" she challenged.

His brows tightened in a scowl, and he stuffed his hands in his pockets, but he spoke with elaborate politeness when he said, "I don't intend to spread details indiscriminately, because it's a personal matter. But I will tell you what you need to know if you decide to help me."

Okay, she could appreciate discreetness in a man; she just hadn't expected to find it in Chris Bentley. His jacket exuded a faint, not unpleasant scent of damp leather, and the overhead walkway lights jeweled the misty droplets clinging to his dark hair and eyelashes and chiseled the lines of his jaw and cheek-bones. She suspected the lights also served to emphasize her own scruffy appearance; her biking outfit was old jeans, not sleek spandex, and the rain had left her face feeling as if it had been through a dishwasher.

Finally Chris said stiffly, "I don't want to hurt Silver, the other Silver, unnecessarily. Perhaps I'll just consult an etiquette book."

"I'm not sure this is covered in the etiquette books. And perhaps you shouldn't place too much value on my opinion of the letter anyway." Silver hesitated. "If you want to know the truth, you were right."

"Right?"

"About my having been dumped. It wasn't recent, but there were certain similarities to your situation, which may have colored my reaction to the letter."

He didn't, as she halfway expected, gloat about his right-ness. He simply asked curiously, "You mean he also sent an inappropriate, business-style letter terminating the relation-ship?"

"It was a breezy note, actually." She paused. She'd been so hurt when it happened, but, after all this time, she could see the situation from a different perspective now. "He wrote it on the back of a birthday card decorated with bluebirds and a rainbow and a poem about this being a wonderful day."

Chris groaned. "That's awful."

Unexpectedly, Silver found herself laughing over the fact that Brad could have done something so carelessly absurd. Chris stayed sober-faced for a moment, but then he laughed, too.

"Did he end it with *cordially?*" he asked.

"He used *arrivederci.* Misspelled."

Chris shook his head. "Do you suppose that somewhere

there's a Museum of Insensitive Clods collecting the outpourings of guys like us?" he asked wryly. He tilted his head and gave her a long, speculative look. She felt disheveled and messy, but she didn't see that reflected in his eyes. "I think you're exactly the right person to help me."

Silver tapped the bicycle helmet against her leg as she considered this unlikely request. She also shivered, the cold and her damp clothes finally combining to send a chill through her.

He reached over and touched her cold hand with his own, warm from the pockets of his sheepskin-lined jacket. "You're freezing! Look, I won't keep you out here any longer. You think about this, and I'll call you in a day or two, okay?"

"Okay."

She was still clutching her door key. Without asking, he took it from her stiff fingers and inserted it into the lock for her. He pushed the door open but made no move to come inside with her, and a minute later she heard the roar of a powerful motorcycle from the parking lot below.

Chris? On a motorcycle? This man was full of surprises.

On Monday morning, while on their coffee break in the employees' lounge, Silver told Colleen about Chris Bentley's explanation for the misguided letter and his strange request.

Colleen clapped her hands delightedly. "Oh, yes, do it! How wonderfully romantic."

"*Romantic?*"

"Yes. You help him out of a bad relationship. You do it with charm and understanding. He sees how sweet and wonderful you are and falls madly in love. It will be a fantastic story to tell your children."

Silver rolled her eyes. So far she'd spilled hot espresso on Chris Bentley, called him an insensitive clod, and clobbered him with a bicycle helmet, and Colleen had them producing a family. "What happened to your earlier label of Mr. Iceberg of the Year?" she inquired.

"So he wrote an iceberg-ish letter." Colleen, with an airy wave of one hand, dismissed that as a hasty judgment. "He can't be too bad if he's willing to ask for help. If a man is a total jerk, he wouldn't recognize insensitivity even with diagrams. He also wouldn't care. And apparently Chris Bentley does recognize it, now that you've kindly pointed it out to him, and does care."

True, Silver granted, although Chris would probably reject *kindly* as the proper word to describe how she'd pointed things out to him. Not that any of this mattered to her on a personal level, of course. This little romantic fantasy was strictly in Colleen's head, not hers.

She wavered back and forth on the unlikely request. One part of her said the whole idea was preposterous. But the other part said, *Okay, Ms. Know-it-all, you complained about injustice in how he treated the other Silver; here's your chance to help correct it.*

She still hadn't decided by the time she answered the phone just after ten o'clock Tuesday evening, and there he was.

"Silver?"

She quickly attributed an unexpected flutter of heartbeat to the simple peculiarity of the situation. "Yes."

"This is Chris Bentley. Sorry to call so late. I just got out of a conference."

"That's okay."

"What have you decided?"

She hadn't, so she stalled with, "Well…"

"Look, I realize this is an imposition. Maybe I could make it up to you. Do you like theater? music? sports?"

"Yes, I like them all," she said warily.

"Could you be more specific?"

"Classic comedy in theater, the *Arsenic and Old Lace* sort of thing. Christian contemporary, gospel, and country and western in music. The Sonics."

"Really?" He sounded surprised, and she wondered which item on her list caused that reaction. "The Sonics are out of town this weekend, and I don't know of any good gospel or Christian contemporary groups in town at the moment, but Reba McEntire is giving a concert at the Tacoma Dome in a couple of weeks."

"I know. All sold out." Not that she could afford the megadollar ticket price for this country-and-western superstar anyway.

"Mrs. Oliver is very good at that sort of thing. I'll ask her to try to locate a couple of tickets."

He was asking her out? Did he think dangling the carrot of a date with him would influence her decision? Silver ruffled with indignation. The ego of the man!

Another thought interrupted. Did she want to go out with him? The sweet shiver that suddenly danced up her spine astonished her. Where had *that* come from?

Then he said, "That way you can take a friend and enjoy yourself."

Silver gulped out, "Thank you," glad he couldn't see the error of her thinking blazed across her face like a swallowed sunset. He might be trying to bribe her, but he wasn't planning personal involvement in a date to do it. She rejected an unexpected letdown feeling.

Okay, she'd take the carrot, she decided. Why not? Fair payment for services performed. "Okay, I'll do it," she said briskly. "But I won't write the letter for you. I'll just make suggestions."

"That's all I expect. Perhaps we could meet at that same

65

espresso shop? I'm tied up with a business dinner tomorrow night, but I should be free by eight-thirty Thursday evening?"

Her calendar was not nearly so full as his. "Yes, I can make that."

Silver, equipped with pen and paper, walked into the espresso shop at eight-twenty Thursday evening. It was considerably more crowded than the last time she had been there, fragrant with the usual tantalizing scents of coffee and hints of cinnamon and vanilla. She carried her almond-flavored latte to a corner table.

Eight-thirty came and went. Eight-forty-five as well. By nine o'clock she'd almost decided he wasn't coming. She was trying to decide if this had all been some cheap payback stunt to inconvenience her—although at the same time troubled by contrasting visions of skidding motorcycle or pickup accidents—when he rushed through the door.

He came straight to the table. "Sorry I'm late. I got hung up at a meeting and couldn't get away."

The first two times she'd seen him she'd been surprised he hadn't looked as she assumed the owner of a chain of motels would look. Tonight he looked every inch of it. Classic-fitting dark suit that brought out that edging of midnight blue in his eyes, crisp pale blue shirt, silvery gray-and-burgundy-striped tie, hair rumpled just enough to show that this was the real, working Chris Bentley, not some clothes jock who couldn't let a mirror go by without checking for perfection. Handsome enough to attract any woman within binocular range, magnetic enough to alter compasses, powerful enough to buy and sell anyone in the room.

And she was going to advise this guy how to handle his private life?

In her dusty-pink leggings and cable-knit tunic she wasn't as scruffy looking as on their earlier encounters, but she certainly wasn't dressed up. She realized her mouth was hanging open. She snapped it shut. "I was going to give you five minutes more."

"I appreciate that. Would you like something to eat?" He motioned toward the sandwich counter. "I'm going to get a sandwich."

"Thanks, no. But I could use another almond latte."

While he was getting the sandwich and hot drinks, she arranged the pen and paper on his side of the table. He returned, set her latte in front of her, and took a sip of his own espresso.

"A brave move, hot espresso, considering your previous experience with me in that area," she suggested with a rueful smile.

"I'm hoping we're meeting under less hostile circumstances this time. But I did include a rather large supply of napkins, just in case of emergencies." He nodded toward what was indeed an oversupply of paper napkins that he'd placed within easy reach. He polished off the smoked turkey sandwich with a few man-sized bites and eyed the pen and paper she'd supplied. He grinned. "So, what comes first? I write 'I am an insensitive clod' five hundred times?"

She couldn't do anything less than smile back at that infectious grin. "You learn fast. But you can do that as a homework assignment."

"I do appreciate your doing this. Before we get started—" He opened his jacket, pulled two tickets from an inner pocket, and handed them to her— "To the Reba McEntire concert. Tacoma Dome, a week from Friday. Should be a terrific concert."

"Your Mrs. Oliver is good," Silver said, impressed. "But perhaps you should wait until we're through to see if I earn this reward."

"I have full confidence in you. I'm going to come out of this the new and improved Chris Bentley." That appealing grin again.

"Okay, the first thing is that you do not dictate this letter to a secretary, even one who handles most personal matters for you. No woman wants to realize that the end of a relationship has been filtered through even one company staff member. Okay?" She waited for his nod before going on. "And handwritten would be preferable because it's more personal."

"Is a special pen required? An egret feather perhaps?" His teasing smile softened the facetious question.

"If you happen to have one lying around," she answered, straight-faced. "Otherwise, an ordinary ballpoint will do."

He pulled a folded paper out of his pocket and handed it to her. "This is the personal stationery the letter should have been written on. Does it pass inspection?"

The paper was a warm beige decorated with a narrow, saddle brown border of small geometric shapes, his name and address in discreet script in one corner, the entire effect masculine yet friendly. It wouldn't have made that original curt letter acceptable, but it would certainly have been a more appropriate setting than the business letterhead. "Yes, I think that will be fine."

He picked up the pen she'd provided, then set it down. "About my not doing this in person and your saying that hiding behind a letter was cowardly and wimpy—I'd like to explain."

"That was perhaps another of my too-harsh judgments. And also none of my business."

"Not doing it in person may very well be cowardly and wimpy," he conceded, as if this were a point he'd already argued with himself. "But I wanted to do it in a letter because in person my resolve might…well, weaken. And that would be a mistake."

Tears, Silver realized. He was afraid that in person, if the other Silver cried, he wouldn't be able to go through with it. Which, unexpectedly, raised her opinion of him. A man who could be affected by tears did have a certain sensitivity. But all she said was, "Fine. The first thing I need to know is why you're breaking up with this other Silver. Another woman?" she asked bluntly.

"No! Of course not. We weren't engaged, but it was an exclusive relationship. I wouldn't cheat on her."

"She did you wrong?"

"No. Silver is a sweet and wonderful woman, loyal and considerate and generous. She comes up from Portland at least once a month to look after her elderly aunt here in Seattle. She's a devoted mother—"

"Mother?" That was a surprise Silver hadn't anticipated.

"She's a widow and has a five-year-old son, Tyler. And her deep faith in God is something to behold."

Another surprise. "Is that a problem?" She'd encountered a few guys like that, men who objected to a woman being "into religion."

"No, definitely not. As a Christian myself, I don't think I could even consider marrying someone who isn't. But just because two people are both believers doesn't mean they'll make good marriage partners." He paused, head tilted as he studied her. And, as Silver could see from the corner of her eye, half the women in the room were studying him. He smiled. "Ah, I see the little wheels whirling. You're thinking, he says he's a Christian, so how come he writes an insensitive-clod letter that sounds as if it were composed by a computer with a hard disk for a heart?"

"The thought crossed my mind," Silver admitted.

He shook his head. "I haven't any good answer for that. I suppose I simply tackled it the way I do any unpleasant task. Start at point A and crash right through to point B."

"A technique that may be an asset in business, but less successful in personal relationships," Silver murmured. "Are you a new believer?"

"It would be convenient if I could say yes, so I just didn't know any better yet, wouldn't it? But I was raised in a Christian family—" He paused, apparently reconsidered that statement, and amended it slightly—"My parents were strong believers, and I made my own commitment to the Lord when I was nine."

Silver smiled, surprised and pleased with this unexpected information. "I was ten," she said softly, "when I gave my heart to Jesus."

She had noted the past-tense mention of his parents, but out of respect for his privacy she didn't inquire further. He studied her so thoughtfully that she felt almost uncomfortable.

"Does it surprise you?" she asked, thinking guiltily of how she'd ripped into him right here at this espresso shop.

"No, not really. I wasn't happy being jumped on about the shortcomings of my letter. But I was impressed that you honestly cared that someone might be hurt and that you had the courage to say so. I suppose all I can say is that, as we both know, Christians make mistakes, too, and what I did here was one of those unfortunate errors." He leaned back in the chair and continued his thoughtful study of her. "What about the guy you were in love with, the one who sent you the birthday-card surprise?"

"I thought he shared my beliefs or I'd never have let myself get so serious about him. But his good-bye note said that he intended to go on to 'explore other areas of spiritual involvement,' as if he'd only been trying on Christianity like a new pair of shoes. The last I heard he was into some New Age, past-life stuff." She sighed but smiled. "The Lord knew he wasn't right for me, but it took me a lot of sleepless nights and a few gallons of tears to get it through my head. Well, we got off the track there, didn't we?" she added briskly. "Back to my original question: Why do you want to break up with the other Silver? She sounds like a real treasure."

"Yeah. She is." He sounded gloomy...or guilty? Then he straightened, removed his jacket, and draped it around the empty chair beside him. "To answer that, I think I should tell you how we got together. I was in Portland meeting with an architectural firm about a remodeling project I was planning on a motel there. One of the men invited me to his home for dinner, so I was driving around an unfamiliar residential area trying to locate the address. In front of me, a car made an unexpected turn and plowed into the side of another car.

"The first car then simply raced off. I stopped to see if anyone in the damaged car was hurt. The little boy was fine, but the woman was unconscious and had a bad gash on her arm. I called an ambulance from a nearby house, and people came running from everywhere. In the confusion, the little boy was somehow left behind, so I took him to the hospital, following the ambulance.

"When we got there, the place was in an uproar because of some big accident on the freeway. I didn't know what to do with Tyler, and his mother, who was Silver, of course, couldn't tell me. I hadn't been around children since I was a kid myself, and I wasn't thrilled to be stuck with one. In fact, I'd have preferred getting my own arm sewed up to the prospect of coping with a strange four-year-old for the next several hours. But I couldn't just abandon him at the hospital, so I called my dinner hosts and explained and stayed."

You could have abandoned him, Silver thought. *Some people would have. But you didn't.*

"Tyler was scared about his mommy being hurt, but he also chattered about everything from a worm he'd found in his backyard to his daddy going to be with Jesus, and we got Fritos

71

and Pepsis from the vending machine, and by the time Silver could go home I was astonished to find I really liked the little guy.

"Silver said they could get a cab, but I took them home. I arranged for a tow truck to take care of her car, and then Tyler and I opened a couple of cans of soup and fixed supper together."

Silver, listening to the story with her chin braced in her hand, smiled. "No wonder she fell in love with you. You charged in like the proverbial knight in shining armor that every girl dreams of."

"That's how she made me feel," he admitted. "Anyway, I was spending several days a month in Portland on the remodeling project, and we started seeing each other regularly. And, as I mentioned before, she comes up here at least once a month to look after her Aunt Louise."

"You kept in touch by phone between visits?"

"Not really. I don't have time for long, chatty phone conversations."

"So you didn't talk on the phone much, and the only times you saw each other were when you happened to be in Portland or she came up here. No special trips just to see each other or do things together?"

"I made a few special trips. For Tyler's birthday or to take him to a ball game or to see a TV character he especially liked."

"What about Silver's birthday? Or special events *she'd* enjoy?"

He tugged at his necktie, as if it had suddenly become too tight, and loosened it an inch. "Being around Silver and Tyler showed me what I was missing in life. The three of us had wonderful fun times together. I began to see us as a family, and it was an appealing picture."

"But?"

"But on the rare occasions when it was just Silver and me, things were…less wonderful. Not that we fought or argued. We didn't. And we both tried our best to accommodate each other and make compromises. I went to a couple of music events she liked. Chamber music, I think it was called. I fell asleep. She tried riding behind me on my motorcycle. She was terrified. She loves chess. I think it's about as interesting as watching fingernails grow. I like skiing and hiking. She prefers a leisurely stroll through a mall or antique store."

"Even the most in-love and compatible couples find they have individual interests that don't appeal to the other person."

"True, and I kept telling myself that. But there just wasn't much of a direct connection between us. Tyler was the center of our relationship. I started looking back on my parents' relationship. We were a wonderfully close family, but there was a connecting link between them that was separate from us boys, something that was just between the two of them. A link—it became more obvious all the time—that Silver and I didn't share." He spoke almost haltingly, as if this were something to which he'd given a great deal of thought but still rather puzzled him. "And eventually I realized all this was unfair to Tyler."

"Unfair?"

"He was putting me in a daddy position in his life, a position I enjoyed. But when he started saying he wanted a baby sister, I knew something had to be done because much as I wanted to be in love with Silver, I just wasn't. I felt an affection for her. I still do. But I couldn't marry her if what I felt wasn't a lifetime kind of love, which also meant I could never be a real daddy to Tyler. And the longer it went on, the more he was going to be hurt eventually." He paused. "Actually, I'd probably have ended the relationship sooner, but Silver decided to open a crafts store specializing in doll-making supplies, and I wanted to help get that going."

His broad chest lifted in a sigh. The sleek tie hung a bit askew now, a tiny flaw in his cosmopolitan look that was oddly appealing. Breaking up with the other Silver had not, as Silver had first assumed, been an unemotional event for him, the act of a man who dumped women as casually as changing stockbrokers. The letter itself had been insensitive, yes. But the motive behind it was not.

"I feel guilty about not being in love with Silver. I feel guilty about breaking up with her. I feel guilty about letting Tyler down."

He pressed his knuckles against his eyes, for a moment looking boyishly vulnerable, and with sudden intuition Silver knew this was more than he'd confided in anyone in a long time. Her hand was halfway across the table to offer a small touch of reassurance, but he opened his eyes, and she curled her fingers around her cup, pretending she'd only been reaching for it.

He picked up the pen and poised it over the blank paper. "So, where do we start?"

"There was nothing wrong with your beginning," she said, and watched as he wrote "Dear Silver" in strong masculine handwriting unlike the signature on the letter, which had been rocker-niece Melissa's, of course.

"My own opinion," she reflected slowly, "is that a letter such as this should let a woman know that the relationship was important, that it was valued, that simply because it is ending doesn't mean that the man is dismissing either her or whatever was between them as insignificant or trivial. A man should let a woman know that he cherishes the memories. A good-bye letter should leave her feeling good about both herself and him. It should convey regret and a bit of nostalgia but also make clear that this is the way things should and must be."

Chris tossed the pen on the table and reared back in his

chair. "Lady, you're asking for a combination of the passion and tenderness of Elizabeth Barrett Browning, the literary skill of Shakespeare, and the wisdom of Solomon!"

Silver didn't deny that. "I think she should cry over losing you but at the same time see the poignant inevitability of it."

"This isn't going to be easy."

"No one said it was," Silver granted. "But isn't she worth it?"

He nodded slowly. "Yes, she is. I want her to know how much the relationship has meant to me. How knowing both her and Tyler has affected me."

"So tell her that."

After a few moments of hesitation he started writing, the bold, masculine scrawl filling the page with surprising speed.

"But now how do I tell her why I'm ending the relationship?"

"Why are you ending it?"

He looked at her as if frustrated by her mental density. "I've just spent the last ten or fifteen minutes telling you about my complicated feelings for both her and Tyler—"

"Cut to the bottom line."

"I love her and Tyler. I really do. But it isn't the becoming-one kind of love that a man and woman share for a lifetime commitment." He paused, troubled. "And yet, because of Tyler, I don't see how we can have an ongoing, just-friends sort of relationship, either. He wouldn't understand. He wants and needs a real daddy."

This was an insight Silver appreciated. She nodded. "Yet you don't want to be enemies, or you wouldn't be doing this." She smiled gently. "So just tell her all that."

He wrote several lines, crossed them out, and started again. He went back to the beginning and turned the paper sideways to insert a line along the edge of the paper, an arrow indicating where it went.

Finally he pushed the paper, filled with changes and crossed-out words and lines, across the table to her, and she read what he had written. It was sweet but never slipped into syrupy; it spoke of joys shared over the past year but evaded sloppy sentimentality. And the parting, the good-bye, was gentle but definite.

"How are you going to close it?" she asked.

He tilted his head thoughtfully. "'With fond memories'?"

She smiled. "Perfect."

He added the line, folded the paper carefully, and tucked it into the inner pocket of his jacket. "I'll do a legible version at home and get it off in the mail tomorrow."

"'Our work here is done, then,'" Silver proclaimed, quoting a character from some old television show. She slipped into her jacket, gathered the leftover paper, and stood up. "Thanks for the tickets."

"I hope you enjoy the performance. And thank you for helping and guiding me."

They looked at each other awkwardly. There was nothing more to say, no reason not to end the meeting now, yet Silver felt oddly reluctant to do so and sensed the same feeling in him.

"Another latte?" He sounded hopeful.

She hesitated. "Thanks, no. I've already had enough." She was awash in latte now.

"Okay. Well, thanks again."

On the way out to her car, Silver fingered the tickets in her pocket. Whom should she invite to accompany her to the concert? She wouldn't lack eager applicants, of course, once friends and relatives knew she had an extra ticket. A bigger problem might be hurt feelings in all those she didn't invite.

At her car, she paused and glanced back through the glass wall of the espresso shop. Chris had taken the letter out of his pocket, apparently to fine-tune a last word or two. A strand of dark hair fell across his forehead as he bent over the letter in concentration, and a totally unexpected thought suddenly surged into her mind.

She scoffed at it, rejected it, tentatively reconsidered. Why not? She could just step back inside for a moment, casually suggest to him—

He glanced up, caught her watching him, tilted his head questioningly.

She instantly abandoned the brief thought. This evening had been pleasant enough. She'd enjoyed it, actually. He wasn't the hard-hearted insensitive clod she'd originally labeled him; he was trying to do the right thing in an awkward situation. He was also fun, personable, attractive. But it had been purely a business deal, nothing more. Assistance asked for, assistance given, assistance paid for with expensive tickets. End of transaction.

She gave him an awkward little wave. He returned it. She got in her car and drove away. Out of sight, out of mind, she told herself firmly.

Not exactly.

Seven

Chris leaped into Silver's mind with the annoying frequency of an obnoxious TV commercial. She was busy with various projects, working the crisis-line phone, giving a talk to a class of eighth-graders about responsible money and credit management, checking to see how Karyn Anderson was doing with her in-law problems, writing a letter about a thoroughly obnoxious ad on TV. But the sight of a rough, muddy pickup instantly reminded her of Chris. So did passing Tommy's Espresso, or the rich scent of perking coffee, or the roar of a motorcycle.

She mentally chastised herself every time she thought about him. Although, thinking about him didn't mean she was *interested* in him, she assured herself. She was merely curious. Curious, too, about this other woman with the same name as her own.

Colleen's husband was going out of town on business the following weekend, so Silver invited a delighted Colleen to attend the Reba McEntire concert with her. But at closing time on Thursday Colleen apologetically said her husband had just called, the business trip was off, and he wanted to take her out to the San Juan Islands for the weekend instead.

"And not even Reba McEntire can compete with a romantic getaway weekend with my husband," Colleen said.

Silver agreed, and that evening, after giving various candidates consideration, called her sister in Renton to offer the extra ticket to her. Marcia groaned at missing this chance, but they'd invited her husband's boss for dinner, and that couldn't be canceled. After several more calls to friends, with rejections ranging from a sick dog to a daughter's piano recital, Silver tapped her fingers on the desk in her tiny living room in vexed frustration.

This was unbelievable. Free tickets to a Reba McEntire concert, and she couldn't find anyone to go with her.

Cousin Dale, she decided finally. He was a really nice guy, although they had so little in common that conversation tended to fizzle into a discussion of the weather when they were together. But just as her finger was poised to dial Dale, the phone rang.

She recognized the male voice even before it got past the beginning, "Hi, Silver," to add, "This is Chris Bentley."

"Hi." She wavered between wariness and a little flurry of excitement.

"I just wanted to let you know I had a note from the other Silver today. She received my letter."

"Was she very upset or angry?"

"No. She was quite understanding. She thanked me for writing such a sweet letter—those were her exact words—and said she appreciated my thoughtfulness and honesty."

"I'm glad to hear that."

"Then she surprised me by saying that she'd been thinking along these same lines herself and was grateful to me for handling the situation so considerately. So I thank you again for your help." He laughed lightly. "I suppose you know *thoughtful* and *considerate* aren't words I'm accustomed to hearing about myself."

"So everything worked out for the best for both of you."

"Yes, I think so."

Still, something in his voice made Silver ask, "Are you sorry you did it?"

"No. It was the right thing to do." He was silent for a long moment, and now she got a definite hint of a letdown or loose-ends feeling that he apparently hadn't anticipated. Feelings that he perhaps wasn't admitting to himself even though he sounded as if he could use cheering up.

The tickets were right by the phone. She was fingering them even as she talked to him. Mentally leaping over her previous rejection of this very idea, she asked impulsively, "Would you like to go to the Reba McEntire concert with me tomorrow night?"

"You don't already have plans to go with someone?" He sounded surprised.

She didn't explain, partly because she didn't want to make him feel like a last-choice companion, partly because she didn't want to incriminate herself as a no-date loser. "No."

"Well, let's see, my calendar shows a business-association dinner—I'll skip it," he added decisively. "How about dinner together before the concert?"

In surprise, she realized he sounded as if the invitation to the concert had indeed cheered him. But dinner? That some-how made more of an event of the evening than she felt comfortable with. "No, I don't think I can make dinner. But we'll have to leave fairly early to allow time for the drive down to Tacoma and parking and finding our seats."

"I'll pick you up, oh, say, six o'clock, then?"

"I could meet you somewhere so you wouldn't have to drive all the way over here."

"I have to go out to the construction site at Bothell tomorrow, so I'll probably come direct to your place from there. If you don't mind riding in the pickup—?"

"I like riding in pickups."

"Really? We'll have to discuss that."

In spite of the vastness of the Tacoma Dome, the sights and sounds of the spectacular show filled the building to every corner. It was a high-energy, firebrand performance of blazing talent, glittering spotlights, video screens, laser effects, and costume changes from black leather to red sequins. And over it all soared Reba's fantastic voice and flamboyant red hair.

The lights still flickered in a dazzling afterglow in Silver's eyes as she and Chris made their way with the slow flow of the crowd toward the exit after the show ended, the final applause still vibrating in her ears.

"Well, what did you think?" Chris kept his hand securely wrapped around hers so the crowd could not separate them.

"Exciting. Exhilarating. I still feel a little breathless!"

She also was grateful to get outside, where even the exhaust fumes from the hundreds of cars in the parking lot couldn't quite overwhelm a definite sea scent in the air. When they reached the pickup, Chris suggested that rather than battle the traffic they just sit and wait for a few minutes until the big parking lot cleared.

"I'm surprised," Silver said. "I didn't think you were the patient type."

Chris laughed. "It doesn't come easily, I admit. But occasionally I grit my teeth and remind myself that what looks like the slow route can sometimes be the fastest in the long run. Besides, now I can ask you about your strange comment that you like riding in pickups."

Silver tucked one leg under her on the wide bench seat with saddle-blanket-style seat covers. There was a comfortable coziness about the dark cab lit only by the parking-lot lights. "Gives me a back-home feeling, I guess. I grew up in a little town in Idaho, and my Dad and two brothers always had pickups. Dad is a dentist, but our home was, and still is, for that matter, several miles out of town on a gravel road, and sometimes a four-wheel-drive pickup is all that can get through the mud and snow."

"Living over here, you don't see your family often, then?"

"A sister and a cousin live in this area, and I try to get home for a visit a couple times a year. We're planning a big family reunion for my parents' thirtieth wedding anniversary in June. How about you? You have family nearby?"

"My brother and his wife live in Montana. He's pastor of a small church there. My parents and grandmother are dead. Ben, my grandfather, recently had to give up living by himself. The doctors think he may be in the early stages of Alzheimer's disease. But, as you may know, its diagnosis is a rather inexact science. He's forgetful, sometimes disoriented, but sometimes I think its a disappointment with life rather than a disease. He lives in a private home now. Usually he knows me when I visit, but there are times when he seems rather vague about who I am."

Chris spoke matter-of-factly, with no indication that he felt his life lacking in family contacts, but it sounded like a rather lonely situation to Silver. She might not see much of her large, extended family, but they were there, no more than a phone call away, if she needed them. A little awkwardly she said, "I'm sorry about your grandfather. It must be difficult, seeing a loved one deteriorate."

"I don't visit him as often as I should, I suppose."

Silver couldn't tell if the faint scowl lines on Chris's face came from sadness about his grandfather's condition or from guilt over not visiting more often. He made no abrupt detour to change the conversation, but she had a feeling this was a subject he'd rather not discuss. With hasty brightness, she said, "Your brother—is he older or younger than you?"

"Five years younger." He laughed, the faint scowl clearing. "And a terrible tease. He calls me the Mighty Motel Mogul."

Silver laughed too. "Sounds appropriate."

By now there were large gaps in the lineup of cars around them. Chris started the engine and eased into traffic straggling out of the parking lot. He turned on the radio, its soft music soothing after Reba's high-octane performance. The heater also blew a welcome blast of warm air against Silver's cold feet.

"Would you mind if we stopped and got a bite to eat somewhere? I was late getting away from the construction site and missed dinner."

"No, of course I wouldn't mind," Silver said quickly. Although curiosity made her ask, "What if I'd taken you up on your invitation for dinner before the concert?" He'd been late arriving at her apartment, giving her ten minutes to wonder if he was going to show up at all.

"I probably wouldn't have gotten there in time for dinner," he admitted.

"Does the word *workaholic* mean anything to you?" Her smile softened her words.

"It should. My brother has explained it to me often enough." He paused and tossed a rueful smile across the dimly lit cab. "As have several women, although the words they used were sometimes less polite than *workaholic* when I was late or missed a date."

"Including Portland Silver?"

"She was always too sweet to complain, but she once served me cold scalloped potatoes and meat loaf as a small example of what happens when a man shows up three hours late without calling."

Silver laughed. "Good for her."

On the outskirts of Seattle he turned off the main highway and stopped at a small café with the blunt announcement of "Jerry's Eats" blazed in red neon across the front. Silver hadn't intended to eat anything, but the scent of sizzling hamburgers tempted her into ordering one.

They sat at a scarred wooden table with chairs to match. The jeans and heavy boots Chris had worn to the concert, direct from tromping around the construction site, would have been out of place in some settings, but here they fit right in. And looked fantastic on his rugged frame.

After he'd taken the edge off his appetite with a few big bites of hamburger, plus a handful of fries smothered in catsup with a squirt of mustard added...ah, a man after her own heart!...Silver asked if he was a Seattle native.

"No, I was born in the Midwest, where my father was pastor of a small church. Later, after he entered the mission field, we lived in Guatemala and then Brazil. But my brother and I returned to live with our grandparents and go to school here in Seattle. After high school, I took some night courses at the university, but I was never really a college student."

Silver smiled. "Too busy becoming a Mighty Motel Mogul?"

He answered her gentle tease with his own smile. "I suppose. But my brother Brian went on to college and studied for the ministry. He has a real gift for reaching people with God's Word."

There was no missing the pride about his brother in Chris's voice, and as he went on to tell her that the brother and wife were expecting their first child in the fall, she suspected he'd rather talk about his brother than himself.

"Did you put your brother through college and studying for

the ministry?" she asked impulsively.

"Well, I...helped." He sounded uncomfortably self-conscious, and she strongly suspected he'd done considerably more than "help" finance his brother's education.

The minibiography he'd given her sounded complete enough, she reflected as she sipped her coffee. Yet there were odd, fractional breaks between the sentences, not his usual manner of speaking. It was almost as if he were editing information as he went, perhaps making flying verbal leaps over important gaps. What kind of gaps?

She dismissed the thought. She should be grateful he wasn't like a guy she'd once dated who thought every minute of his life, from a traumatic experience with a pet turtle at age six to how he'd told the boss off yesterday, was so fascinating that it must be related in minute detail. She was curious about Chris's life as a missionary kid, but before she could ask, he had a question of his own.

"I'm curious. How does one become a credit counselor?"

"In my case, it started with a credit mess of my own," Silver admitted. "I went to the University of Idaho for two years but didn't have any concrete goal in mind, so I dropped out to work. I came to Seattle mostly because my sister lived in the area. I got a job in a ski and scuba shop...odd combination, right? But they're both sports I love."

"Really? Maybe we can do one or both together sometime. There are some fascinating diving areas around the San Juan Islands."

"That may be beyond my amateurish abilities," Silver admitted. "The only places I've dived have been in a swimming pool and a shallow lake. I didn't get any further than that before I lost my equipment."

He glanced up, the last bite of his hamburger halfway to his mouth. "Lost?"

"No dramatic diving accident," she said wryly. "Lost as in repossessed."

He smiled, not unsympathetically. "Oh. I see."

"All that expensive equipment was the beginning of my personal downfall. I was surrounded in the shop by all these tantalizing, high-priced toys, which I could buy at an employee discount, and I'd be foolish not to take advantage of such a terrific opportunity, right?" She shook her head at her own blithely naïve attitude. "I'll bet you never did anything like that."

"I've never been much for buying things on credit," he agreed, "but I've taken some big financial chances and plunged deep into debt on various motel-buying and expansion deals." He paused. "Actually, I'm about to take another big plunge now."

Silver was curious what that meant, but he didn't offer details, and she went on with her own story. "Anyway, with established credit, I started getting credit-card offers, and I grabbed them all. I got a different apartment and furnished it on credit. Getting a new car on credit was easy, too.

"Then I also had some large, unexpected dental bills. And first thing I knew, it just snowballed. I started a juggling act using one credit card to pay off another, dreading the mail or the phone because it was sure to be another angry creditor. About that time the partners in the store had a big blowup, and I lost my job in the split. So then I was *really* in financial trouble.

"The juggling act collapsed. Stuff started getting repossessed. My landlord threatened to evict me because I couldn't pay my rent." She smiled ruefully. "I started wondering if the dentist could repossess my unpaid dental work."

She shook her head. She could laugh a little about her foolishness now, but she remembered how out of control and helpless and panicky she'd felt, as if water in a closed aquarium were rising around her, and her head was about to go under. "I suppose my folks would have bailed me out, but I figured I'd gotten myself into this mess and I'd better get myself out. I went to Wintergreen Credit Counseling for help, and then I wound up going to work for them as a receptionist. Later I took some college courses and other training and passed a test to become a certified counselor myself."

"I'll bet you're good at it, too."

Silver nodded with modest pride. "I think I am. I've been there, so I know how easy it is to fall into the credit trap. I feel a real empathy for those who have also tumbled into it. Though I sometimes get the impression that our new office manager wonders how people could be so stupid and irresponsible to get in the financial messes they're in." She hesitated. "I love my work, helping people find their way back to solid ground financially, but sometimes I'm frustrated by my limitations in helping them."

"Limited how?"

"I see people whose real problem is a desperate need of the Lord, but all I can do is help them with credit problems. Rules and regulations. I wish I could start a Christian counseling service that could tackle a whole array of personal problems, credit and finances, marriage, children, employment, and spiritual problems, too, of course, because they're so often intertwined."

"So do it."

"It isn't that simple," she said, although his go-for-it words didn't really surprise her. That was obviously how he did things. "It takes financing and experience and organization. I don't have any fancy degree with which to impress people."

"So get one."

"That could take years!"

"The years will go by anyway." He smiled as he said it, but it was obvious that he was serious. "But a first step might be looking for employment with a Christian counseling service."

"I checked into that with a couple of organizations, but they weren't dealing directly with credit and finance problems, negotiating with creditors and helping people set up workable repayment plans as we do, so there weren't any job openings."

"So convince one of them they need to add a credit counselor to deal specifically with those problems. Make an opening for yourself."

"Spoken like a man who crashes directly from point A to point B, letting nothing get in his way." But convincing a Christian counseling service to add such a position was an interesting thought, she had to admit.

At the apartment complex he took her hand lightly as they walked up to her second-floor door. Here the fir trees lining the parking area scented the night air with a damp, evergreen freshness and muted the sounds of city traffic. She put her key in the lock.

He leaned against the wall beside the door, feet crossed at the ankles. "How do you feel about motorcycles?"

"Are you trying to sell me one?"

He laughed. "No."

"I took a dim view of them for a while after my brother dumped us both in a ditch with one when we were teenagers."

"That soured you on motorcycles?" He sounded disappointed.

Silver smiled. "No, it made me learn to ride one by myself, so I wouldn't have to ride behind and depend on him."

"How about a motorcycle ride with me on Sunday afternoon? Perhaps out to Snoqualmie Falls? It should be spectacular this time of year."

Silver hesitated. A woman asking a man on a first date was theoretically a nineties thing to do. She'd had fun tonight and thought Chris had too. But she still didn't feel totally comfortable with the situation. She decided to be blunt. "Chris, just because I invited you to this concert tonight doesn't mean you're obligated to reciprocate. It wasn't really a...date, anyway."

"Oh? You could have fooled me. We had music, food, conversation, and hand holding." Laughter lurked in his voice as he held up his fingers and ticked off the typical elements of a date, but his tone turned gently serious when he added, "What you're really thinking is that if I'd wanted to go out with you, I'd have asked you first, right?"

Silver managed a noncommittal combination of murmur, shrug, and cough.

"Silver, I thought about asking you out when we were at the espresso shop. But I just wasn't sure I was ready to get involved with anyone so soon after breaking up with the other Silver."

"I can understand that. But I didn't have involvement in mind when I invited you. You just sounded down and discouraged, and I thought—"

"Oh, so it was a pity date."

Silver started to deny that but saw the teasing gleam in his eyes and agreed instead. "Okay, so it was a pity date. I felt so-o-o sorry for the Mighty Motel Mogul."

"Well, whatever it was, I was really pleased when you invited me to the concert because I definitely was feeling a little down. And we won't call Sunday a date, okay? I'll just drop over after church, about one-thirty, and if you're here and would like to go, fine. And if not, that's fine too."

Silver hesitated, but she didn't have to make up her mind now, of course. "Okay. I'll think about it."

Eight

$\mathcal{S}$ ilver wavered back and forth about accepting Chris's invitation, although she wasn't certain why. A motorcycle ride sounded like fun, and she'd never seen Snoqualmie Falls. Of course it could pour down rain on Sunday afternoon, and that wouldn't be much fun on a motorcycle. Except that she could imagine laughing and enjoying herself in the rain with Chris even if they were getting drenched.

Aha! she thought with a jolt of discovery that was part triumph, part dismay. She was in the shower, washing her hair, a cloud of apple-blossom scent from her favorite herbal shampoo floating around her. There it was, the real reason she was hesitating. It was because she *could* imagine having a marvelous time with Chris, no matter what the uncomfortable circumstances.

Why should that be disturbing? Because she could also peer farther down the trail and see the definite possibility of her feelings for Chris growing stronger, much stronger. And seeing even more clearly that falling for a guy on the rebound, which Chris definitely was, whether he realized it or not, was a good way to get your heart broken.

Okay, that was settled, she told herself briskly as she bent at the waist and toweled her hair damp-dry before turning on the blow dryer. She just wouldn't be here on Sunday afternoon when he arrived. This didn't necessarily mean she was closing the door on him permanently, she reminded herself to quiet an internal rumble of protest. Perhaps later, when he was definitely out of the rebound woods, they could make a fresh connection.

Yet on Sunday morning, she found herself getting up early to bake chocolate-chip cookies—scraping the bottoms off the half that burned—and make tuna sandwiches and a tangy pasta salad. She placed everything on the bottom shelf of the refrigerator and then stared at the cluster of plastic containers with a certain grumpy consternation.

What was going on here? She'd decided against going with Chris, but this definitely looked like a picnic for two. Complete with homemade cookies. *Homemade cookies.* She hadn't made cookies for any guy since Brad.

She got Chris off her mind during the sermon and joyful singing, but he was back again as she headed home after church, a little late because she'd stopped to talk with Hank Arlands about a meeting of the summer-camp committee. She realized she was attacking the gas pedal as if the street were a drag strip and forced herself to let up on it. No need to hurry. True, the day was perfect for a motorcycle ride, all sunshine and blue sky, the air unseasonably balmy. But it was also just as fine a day for a solo bicycle ride.

But she was home well before one-thirty. She also had the lunch packed in a sack with a thermos filled with coffee and was dressed in jeans, an old pair of heavy hiking boots, and a light shell blouse under a heavier denim shirt. She was just dropping a hooded jacket beside the lunch when the doorbell rang.

Chris grinned, dark hair rumpled from his motorcycle helmet, at the moment looking much more like a handsome heart-breaker than a Mighty Motel Mogul. "Somehow I thought you'd stand me up."

"You can't stand someone up if it isn't really a date," she pointed out. She still felt grumpy with herself for doing this, as if her better judgment had been hijacked by...what? Her heart? No, not her heart. She liked Chris, but her heart certainly wasn't involved. At least not yet. But there was that definite—and dangerous—glimmer of *possible* involvement of the heart.

Yet by the time they got out to the parking lot, the mouth-watering prospect of a motorcycle ride on this glorious day was enough to tell her she was making too much of this, that it was, after all, just a motorcycle ride, not a doomsday adventure into heartbreak.

"Gold Wing!" she exclaimed when she saw the big, sleek machine, fully dressed with saddlebags and trunk, the chrome and berry wine color shimmering in the sun.

"I take it you know a little about motorcycles." His helmet, plus the one he dug out of the trunk for her, were that same rich color.

She knew enough to recognize that this elegant machine probably cost double the price of her used compact car. "My brother over in Spokane, the unmarried one, has an older Gold Wing." Not in this price range, however.

"The same brother who dumped you in the ditch?" Chris asked as he stowed the lunch and thermos in the trunk.

"The same one." Silver fastened the strap of the helmet under her chin and adjusted the dark-tinted face shield. "He'd trip over his own tongue drooling over this bike."

"Maybe I'll get to meet him sometime, and he can take it for a spin."

It was a throwaway line, no different than the socially mean-ingless, *We'll have to get together sometime.* But it gave Silver the definite impression that Chris was perhaps peeking into future possibilities between them, an impression that suddenly made the sun feel warmer and the sky bluer.

Chris swung his leg over the motorcycle, long legs and lean body easily holding the heavy machine upright, and she stepped into the curved, richly padded seat behind him. "Ready?" he asked over his shoulder.

"Ready."

"Okay if we go by way of Bothell? I need to check on something at the construction site."

Somehow she wasn't surprised that he was sneaking in a bit of side-trip business, that he couldn't totally commit himself to getaway fun even for an afternoon, but she offered no objections. "Fine by me."

They headed east over the Evergreen Point floating bridge, then north to Bothell. The new motel was impressive even in the raw construction stage, a big sign proclaiming it the newest addition to Maraben Inns. Silver waited at the motorcycle while Chris went around back. Then they took a scenic back route to Snoqualmie Falls, a two-lane road winding through lush green trees, with a surprising number of big homes almost hidden from sight here and there in the thick foliage.

Silver hadn't been on a motorcycle in several years, and she loved the glorious rush of country air flowing around her, the delightful pockets of warm and cool air unnoticed when riding in a car, the delicious swoop around curves with the road only inches below her feet, the earthy, close-up scents of fields and forests. Plus the wonderful scent of sun-kissed leather enclosing her partner on the motorcycle.

Snoqualmie Falls lived up to all the praise she'd heard of it. The observation point was almost on a level with the falls that plunged in a silver-white avalanche to the river some 270 feet below, 100 feet more than the drop of Niagara Falls. A fine spray floated up, coating faces and hair and clothing with a cool mist, and a dramatic thunder of falling water roared in their ears. The unseasonably warm day had brought out a big crowd of people, and Chris kept hold of Silver's hand as they strolled around viewing the falls from different points along the walkway.

They were just spreading their jackets on a grassy spot for lunch when a stray Frisbee hit Chris on the shoulder. A little boy ran up, followed by a younger look-alike who had to be a brother.

"We're, uh, sorry," the older boy muttered as both boys looked big-eyed at Chris, obviously not knowing what to expect from this rugged, intimidating-looking man now in possession of their Frisbee.

Silver didn't know what to expect from Chris either. But suddenly he took several steps backward and flashed her a grin. "Catch!"

Silver caught. For a moment the boys looked confused, but Silver instantly caught on and remembered a silly, singsong ditty from her own Frisbee-throwing days as a kid. "We throw high, we throw fast, we'll be first, and you'll be last!" she challenged. By now Chris was well away from the jackets, and she whipped the Frisbee to him with a smooth flip of her wrist.

The little boys exuberantly took up the challenge, and instantly the two adults and two children were playing a wild game of keep away, the Frisbee soaring and swooping like some miniature UFO. With a surprising leap one of the boys snatched the Frisbee in midair, and then Silver and Chris were trying to get it back. The spinning disk changed hands several times before Chris finally laughed and tossed it to the boys.

"Okay, kids. You've worn this old man out." He wasn't even breathing hard from the energetic game, but he made a melodramatic show of collapsing spread-eagle on the jackets, and the boys ran off, giggling.

Silver's collapse beside him was more authentic. Those kids had run her ragged, enjoyably ragged! After she caught her breath, she opened the plastic cartons and spread the lunch between them. "That was fun. I haven't played Frisbee in years."

"Tyler and I play with one once in a while." He paused, and though he didn't say the words, Silver could almost hear them. *Tyler and I used to play with one.* Even unspoken they sounded regretful.

She looked up from the coffee she was pouring from thermos to plastic cup and impulsively said, "Maybe you should reconsider—"

But before she could finish the sentence, he was remarking, in what she was almost certain was a deliberate interruption, "Hey, are these cookies homemade?" Then a bold jay hopped up looking for a handout, and they laughed at his antics. Soon the bird had competition from a couple of frisky squirrels, and then Chris started telling her about a bear that had invaded his ice chest on a camping trip.

"And I was trying to chase him away, but he was not much impressed with the weapon I grabbed, which was the goose-down pillow out of my sleeping bag. Then the pillow broke open, and there I was with about a million feathers flying around, and I swear the only reason that bear didn't come after me was because he was laughing too hard."

Silver laughed too, and they never did get back to discussing whether he should reconsider the breakup. Then she had a story of her own to tell about a family camping trip to a lake in Idaho, when one of her brothers had tried to scare Silver and her sister by pretending to be a bear outside their tent. "But we knew it was him, so we just squirted him with catsup. He howled bloody murder, and my folks rushed out, saw all that catsup, and thought he'd been attacked." She shook her head, and they were both laughing again.

It was almost dark by the time they got back to her apartment, and even in her heavy jacket, the ride was cold enough to make her move stiffly as she dismounted from the motorcycle.

He touched a cold palm to her even colder cheek. "You're icy! Let's get you inside."

Silver hesitated, not quite certain how to end this "non-date." They'd had such fun laughing and playing together, and she didn't want to ruin it with awkward good-byes. "You don't need to come up with me."

"I may have my flaws in the area of sensitivity," he stated, "but I believe in the old-fashioned rule of always seeing a woman to her door." He made a grand flourish of bowing as he motioned her to the apartment stairs.

"Providing you manage to show up at her door to begin with," Silver teased lightly, remembering his admission about forgotten or skipped dates.

He grinned ruefully. "True."

At her door he put an arm around her shoulders and squeezed lightly, a gesture more companionable than romantic. "I've enjoyed today. I'm glad we went."

"So am I."

"Maybe we could do something next weekend?"

"Such as?"

"Oh, skiing, bicycling, hiking. Or how do you feel about roller-blading?"

"Sore after the couple of times I tried it," she admitted, remembering some spectacular spills. "But interested."

"Good. I'll give you a call during the week, then, and we'll decide what we want to do."

Chris did call, but only to say he had to go out of town on business over the weekend. He wasn't specific, but she gathered the trip was connected with the big financial "plunge" he had in the works. But the following Saturday they went bicycling together along Lake Washington, having the wet bike trail under dripping trees almost to themselves. He did not pedal leisurely, which did not surprise her and which also suited her fine; she'd ridden with people who frustrated her with their dilatory approach. But they also stopped to skip rocks on the calm, rain-speckled lake, share a mangled old candy bar he found in his jacket pocket, and watch a jet skier circling on the water.

"I've been thinking about trying that one of these days," Chris said.

"Me, too."

And they looked at each other and grinned like two children contemplating mischief together.

"But it was pouring down rain on Saturday!" Colleen said when Silver told her on Monday morning about bicycling with Chris. "You must have been freezing."

"No, it was fun," Silver insisted. "And then we stopped for chili afterwards." Which they both liked so spicy hot that their eyes watered while they ate.

"Oh, I see what's happening." Colleen nodded, now a little sly and smug. "What did I tell you? True love is blossoming, because only true love could make bicycling in a miserable, cold rain *fun*."

"No, that isn't it at all," Silver objected instantly. "We're just friends who happen to enjoy some of the same activities. No big romance." She stirred her coffee briskly. Perhaps too briskly, she decided, as she realized Colleen was watching the vigorous spoon whipping with a speculative expression. "They aren't even real dates. We're just doing things together."

"When's your next not-a-real-date with him?"

"If he has time and the snow is still good, we may go skiing next weekend. Or, if the snow's gone, maybe roller-blading."

"A guy who likes all the same sweaty activities you do." Colleen, whose trim figure belied the fact that her idea of exercise was strolling to the nearest taco stand to order cheese-drenched nachos, wrinkled her nose. "Not exactly *my* cup of tea, but perfect for you."

Again Silver protested, "We're just friends."

"Silver, haven't you considered that this may be the man the Lord has in mind for you?" Colleen asked with unexpected seriousness. "Being *friends* is a far better preliminary to love than some wild infatuation or shallow physical attraction. And think about the unlikely way you met! Think about the unlikely circumstance of not being able to find anyone but him to go with you to the Reba McEntire concert. And remember that God moves in mysterious ways."

"And remember that *you* have the world's biggest match-making imagination."

Colleen ignored that. "You say he's a believer. What else do you know about him by now?"

Silver shrugged. "Not a lot." The activities they'd shared so far were not conducive to intimate conversation, although a few disconnected personal facts had surfaced. "He's never heard anything more from the other Silver. He finally got that storm of diaper deliveries stopped. He belongs to a different church than I do, but our Christian beliefs are pretty much the same. He owns a condo over in the Magnolia area." By now she also knew that his big financial plunge involved the takeover of another chain of motels, but she didn't mention that because everything was being kept very hush-hush until the complicated financing was secured and the dotted lines signed. But their time together was really more *doing* than discussing.

"Invite him over for dinner," Colleen advised. "Cook something romantic." She paused and, apparently remembering a certain flaming-dessert fiasco, amended the advice slightly. "But nothing flammable. You want the guy to talk, not yell for the fire department."

Silver just rolled her eyes.

The snow wasn't top-notch, but they went skiing out at Stevens Pass anyway, and Silver wasn't surprised when Chris headed for the steepest, most difficult runs. He obviously played the same way he worked, wide-open and full speed ahead, not carelessly reckless but definitely willing to take chances. Silver kept her speed more in check, but she was an expert enough skier to take the advanced runs with him, and it was an exhilarating day on the slopes.

Yet afterwards, what she remembered wasn't the thrill of flying airborne over a hump of snow or delighting in the skid of a sharp turn. It was the laughter and companionship of the day, the fun of being with Chris, his concerned rush to help her to her feet after an ignominious spill. And his congratulatory kiss on her cheek after one of their more spectacular runs, a small spot that she surreptitiously touched with a kind of shivery wonder every few minutes afterwards because such a special rosy tingle lingered there.

Could she, she asked herself uneasily as she soaked in a tub of hot bubbles that evening, be deceiving both herself and Colleen with her glib claim of just being friends with Chris? Was she poised on the brink of falling in love, like some swirling drop of water just before the plunge over Snoqualmie Falls?

Was it even possible, as Colleen suggested, that this was the man the Lord intended for her? And she for him?

It was a thought that she frequently took out and examined during the next few days, as if it were some exciting treasure box just waiting to be opened.

A thought that she hastily discarded after what happened the following week.

Nine

Apple blossoms.

Chris let the page of projected earnings for the Golden Lighthouse chain drift back against the dining-room table. Yes, that's what the scent was! He'd been trying all week to place the faint fragrance that lingered in his memory, and now he had it. Silver's wild hurricane of blond hair smelled faintly of apple blossoms.

He liked the scent of apple blossoms.

He also liked a woman who didn't mind getting her hair mussed, who wasn't afraid to tell him when he was wrong, who enjoyed the ski slopes and bicycle paths as much as he did.

The phone rang, and he yanked his attention back to business. This should be the late call he was expecting from Dick Richardson, who was negotiating with a lawyer representing the woman on the East Coast who owned a share of the Golden Lighthouse chain.

But it wasn't Dick Richardson on the line.

"Chris, I'm sorry to bother you, but I didn't know what else to do."

He recognized the voice instantly, even though he hadn't

heard it for weeks now. He also heard the uncharacteristic agitation in it. "Silver, is something wrong?"

"It's Aunt Louise. I've been trying to call her since noon. I've left several messages on her answering machine, and it's so unlike her not to call me back. And you know she never stays out this late."

"Have you tried her neighbors?" The elderly people in Aunt Louise's neighborhood had an informal system of checking on each other regularly.

"Her friend Ellie is in California visiting relatives, and I can't rouse Alice Jefferson. I think she's been down with the flu. And Al Striker passed away recently."

Chris glanced at his watch. Ten-thirty. Probably Aunt Louise was safe and sound, or it was possible she had simply stayed out unusually late. But Silver was not some nervous worrywart, and he knew she wouldn't have called unless she was deeply concerned.

A point emphasized when Silver added worriedly, "She's been having some little dizzy spells lately."

"I'll run over and check on her right away. I'll call you back as soon as I can."

He heard her swallow. "Thanks, Chris."

The modest frame house was dark when Chris parked his pickup at the curb. Unusual, right there. Aunt Louise always stayed up until after midnight watching the late TV shows. Although the house would be dark, of course, if she were out late.

No, there was her white Ford parked under the carport.

He rang the front bell. No answer. He went around back. No bell there, but he knocked loudly, hammering the doorframe hard enough to vibrate the wooden steps.

He paused, fist poised for another knock. Was that a noise

from inside? He strained against the screen door, but all he could hear was the faint rustle of a cedar branch brushing against the roof.

There must be a key here somewhere. He checked over the door, under the doormat, and beneath several nearby flowerpots. Nothing. He eyed the window over the kitchen sink. He could break it and climb in if he had to, but surely there was a key here somewhere. He tried to follow Aunt Louise's quirky thought processes about a suitable hiding place.

But when another faint sound—a moan?—came from inside, he grabbed a flowerpot, balanced on the rail beside the steps, and smashed the pot into the kitchen window. He reached through the ragged hole, unfastened the latch, and hoisted himself inside.

He flicked on the kitchen light, blinking momentarily at the dazzling glare. A broken cup lay on the floor by the kitchen sink.

Then he saw her, a crumpled heap on the dining-room floor, and in horror he realized this accident must have happened hours ago because she was still in her morning bathrobe and hair curlers. And apparently she'd been desperately dragging herself across the floor ever since, trying to get to the phone in the living room.

"Aunt Louise!"

He ran to her, but he did no more than touch her throat to check for a pulse before rushing to dial 911. Then he sat beside her, holding her hand, knowing from the unnatural angle of her body that he dare not move her, even to try to make her more comfortable. She moaned again, but the sound came from somewhere beyond her consciousness.

The ambulance arrived in minutes, the attendants expertly transferring her from floor to stretcher to vehicle. He gave them the name of the hospital she'd been in before, when she had

had knee surgery. He dialed the Portland phone number even as they were carrying Aunt Louise out. He heard the strain in Silver's voice when she answered on the first ring. "Chris?"

He jumped up as soon as Silver entered the brightly lit emergency room, taking a sleep-limp Tyler from her tired arms. It was some six hours since he'd called her, but only a faint increase in the tempo of activity around the hospital indicated morning was near, because a steady rain obliterated all signs of a coming dawn.

"Oh, Chris, you didn't have to stay here all this time. But I'm so grateful you did!" Worry and weariness shadowed her eyes, and her usually crisply curling dark hair hung limply around her temples. "I'm sorry I didn't get here sooner, but everything went wrong."

He shifted Tyler to one arm and pulled her close with his other arm, trying to reassure her even as he feared there was little reassurance to offer.

She looked up at him, brown eyes fearful. "Do you know how she is?"

Chris shook his head. "I'm not family, so they wouldn't tell me much. But I know her doctor is here."

He sat on one of the hard plastic chairs with Tyler snuggled against his shoulder while Silver went to the desk for information. The little boy's fair skin looked so fragile, so vulnerable as his small body lay across Chris's lap, so in need of someone strong to protect and cherish him. Chris dropped his cheek to the dark blond head. He'd convinced himself breaking up with Silver was right. But was it?

Silver returned with the information that her aunt's left hip was shattered, and she was in emergency surgery now. Chris knew how devastating such an injury could be. His grandmother had survived only a few days after breaking her hip in a fall.

Silver wiped a knuckle across the tear trickling down her cheek. He could see her pulling herself together, drawing on inner reserves of strength from the Lord. He put a steadying arm around her shoulders.

"You don't need to stay longer, Chris. I know you haven't had any sleep, and I can manage now."

"I'll stay."

He stayed until Aunt Louise was moved from the operating room into intensive care. The doctor said the surgery, which had fastened the bones with several metal pins, had gone satisfactorily, but he was guarded about the patient's prospects for recovery. Chris felt groggy when he went directly to the office, but three cups of coffee had sharpened his mind by the time he conferred with Dick Richardson about problems negotiating with the Golden Lighthouse shareholder. He skipped lunch to talk to a building inspector about a problem with code regulations on the Bothell construction. Then the temporary secretary who was substituting for Mrs. Oliver while she was on vacation informed him that Silver Sinclair had called while he was on the phone.

He hesitated, then asked cautiously, "Which one?"

"Pardon?" The woman, who knew nothing of the odd two-Silvers situation, sounded bewildered by the strange question.

"Never mind. Did she leave a number?"

"No. She just said to tell you she called."

"Okay. Thanks." Under different conditions he supposed the situation might have been humorous: a confused man caught between two attractive women with the same name. But with Aunt Louise's condition so precarious, humor was definitely lacking. After a moment's consideration, he decided the call logically must have come from Portland Silver. Except for that very first call before they actually knew each other, Seattle Silver had never called him, and she probably would have made clear which Silver she was if she had called now.

Silver answered when he dialed Aunt Louise's number, and he quickly apologized for being tied up on another line when she called earlier.

"I didn't call." She sounded surprised.

"You didn't?" He, too, was surprised.

"But I was just about to pick up the phone to call, so maybe it was mental telepathy." She sounded as if she were trying to force a cheerfulness that wasn't there.

She didn't ask for an explanation of why he thought she'd called, but Chris felt awkward and uncomfortable, even a little guilty. Though there was no reason to feel that way, he reminded himself. He hadn't done anything underhanded or unfair to either Silver. But he definitely had to explain the unlikely two-Silvers situation to this Silver soon. For now, however, all he said was, "Have you heard anything about Aunt Louise?"

"I just talked to the hospital. She'll be in intensive care for at least another twenty-four hours. Maybe longer, if things don't...go right. Oh, Chris, she's the only relative Tyler and I have."

For a moment she sounded on the verge of breaking down, and he wished he could reach out and put his arms around her to comfort her, but all he could do at the moment was ask about practical matters. "Is a lot of cold air and rain coming through that broken window?"

"I draped a blanket over it."

"Have you had any sleep? Eaten anything?"

"I lay down for a couple of hours, and I'm fixing a sandwich now."

"Good. Take another nap, and I'll meet you at the hospital about four-thirty. I'll see what I can do with the window after that."

There was a small silence, and then she said, "Chris, none of this is your problem or responsibility. I appreciate your taking care of everything last night. Aunt Louise might have died if you hadn't gotten here when you did. But, under the circumstances..."

"Would you rather I didn't come to the hospital?"

"Oh, Chris, no! I didn't mean that. It's wonderful to have you to lean on. And Tyler can't wait to see you again. He asked about you as soon as he woke up. But..." Again her voice trailed off, and the circumstances stood between them like the open fissure of an earthquake.

Chris determinedly leaped over the fissure. "I'll be there," he promised almost roughly.

He replaced the phone, the thought immediately occurring to him that if this Silver hadn't called, the call must have come from the other Silver. He looked up the Wintergreen Credit Counseling Service in the phone book. A receptionist put him through to Silver's desk.

"Chris, hi," she said, sounding a little harried. "I'm sorry I bothered you at the office, but I don't have your home number."

A bit of an accusation there? Chris wondered. No. Not from what-you-see-is-what-you-get Silver. Simple statement of fact. "That's fine. No problem."

"What I called about—when we went skiing, could I have left my sunglasses in your pickup? I can't find them anywhere, and that's the last time I remember seeing them."

"I'll see if I can find them."

"Thanks. Oh, here comes my next client! Bye."

"Silver—"

But she'd already hung up.

He held the phone for a moment, feeling frustrated that he hadn't had a chance to tell her about the accident and that the other Silver was in town, but he couldn't involve her in a long personal call now if she was with a client. He'd have to talk to her later.

At the hospital, he stayed with Tyler while Silver went in to see Aunt Louise. Silver shook her head when she returned; at this point Aunt Louise was still not recovering properly from the anesthesia. He took them out for the fish and chips that were Tyler's favorite eat-out food and then followed them back to Aunt Louise's house to see what he could do about the window. Not much, as it turned out, although he did reinforce the blanket with a couple of old boards. He tucked Tyler in bed while Silver called her one employee in Portland to discuss what to do about the crafts store. Afterwards, knowing Silver didn't want to be alone, he stayed, drinking coffee and talking, until almost midnight.

By the time he got home he was so tired that he sat down to take off his shoes and woke several hours later to find that he'd fallen asleep right there in the chair. He undressed and stumbled into bed.

The next day was just as hectic, with a sudden demand from the bank for pages and pages of figures and new information on his application to restructure his debt load to handle the Golden Lighthouse purchase. He sent a repairman out to replace the window at Aunt Louise's house and then met Silver at the hospital again, where they waited over an hour for the doctor to arrive and discuss her aunt's prognosis.

Late that afternoon he tried to call Seattle Silver at the credit-counseling office, but she was in a meeting. He finally told his substitute secretary to keep trying until she reached Silver, then tell her that he wouldn't be able to make the hike out at Lake

Sammamish that they'd tentatively planned for Saturday.

"And be sure to tell her I apologize for my not making the call myself," he instructed. Since Silver's insensitive-clod speech, he was more aware of handling personal matters himself. "Tell her an emergency has come up, and I'll explain later."

By Saturday Aunt Louise was in a private room, although her recovery still was not progressing as it should. Chris took Tyler for the day because the little boy was just too lively and active to be cooped up for hours in the hospital room. They went out to the construction site at Bothell, where Tyler was fascinated with the big backhoe scooping out a trench, and then to the Seattle zoo. Chris felt a little guilty for enjoying the day so much, with Aunt Louise lying in the hospital and Silver so upset and worried.

Sunday evening they almost lost Aunt Louise. She was rushed back into intensive care, and Chris and Silver spent most of the night at the hospital, praying and hoping. Tyler spent the night with Louise's neighbor Ellie, who was back from California.

But by Monday afternoon, Aunt Louise was miraculously on the upswing, even smiling weakly when Chris and Silver went to see her. "Maybe it's just knowing that the two of you are together again that's making me feel so much better," she whispered.

Chris and Silver exchanged awkward glances. Nothing was really changed between them, of course.

Or was it?

Ten

"Chris, you don't have to make a special trip just to bring the sunglasses to me tonight," Silver protested into the phone.

"I want to talk to you about something anyway," Chris said.

"Oh. Well, okay, fine." With sudden intuition she knew that the talk, not the return of the sunglasses, was the real reason for this unexpected midweek visit. "See you in a few minutes, then."

How odd, she thought, mentally reviewing the brief phone call after returning to the stove to stir her simmering spaghetti sauce. She hadn't heard anything from Chris for over a week, except for that message from a secretary in his office. Actually, plans for the hike hadn't been all that definite anyway, which was typical of their decidedly casual relationship, and she hadn't been surprised by the call. Chris's attention was so focused on the takeover of the other motel chain that she sometimes wondered if he took time to sleep and eat. But now, all of a sudden, he just had to see her within the next hour. Yes, definitely odd.

Perhaps she should be flattered.

She stopped stirring. Flattered? No, not that. His wanting to "talk" now seemed to hold an ominous undertone. Had something disastrous happened to his important business deal? Or his brother or grandfather?

Yet when he arrived, he didn't appear upset. His smile was normal, his hand steady when he brushed raindrops from his hair, his masculine magnetism at full force. His casual slacks and darker jacket occupied a neutral position somewhere between the killer-sharp suit in which she'd once seen him and the jeans and heavy boots he often wore. He looked, she decided thoughtfully, on his way to somewhere other than *here.*

"Ummm, what's that I smell?" He sniffed appreciatively.

"Spaghetti. Loaded with garlic. Want to stay and eat?"

"No, I guess not. Thanks anyway." He sounded momentarily regretful but briskly turned to the reason for this visit. "I brought your sunglasses. They'd fallen under the seat in the pickup."

He handed the soft, blue fabric case to her, and she thanked him. She was just about to offer coffee when he made the blunt announcement that caused her to clutch the glasses case so hard that something crunched inside. "What did you say?"

"Silver—the other Silver, I mean—and I have decided to get back together."

"Oh. I see." She cast around for something non-inane and nonincriminating to say. Momentarily her mind simply buzzed with meaningless static, like a television screen with a station knocked out by a power outage. "I guess I'm not really surprised," she finally managed. Which was the truth, she realized. She was definitely startled by the unexpected announcement but, on a deeper layer, not surprised.

He shuffled his feet in a manner uncharacteristic of his usual self-assurance. "I feel awkward about this, but I wanted to tell you in person."

"No need to feel awkward! I once went to a wedding, stepped on the bride's train, and ripped it half off. Now *that's* awkward."

He smiled appreciatively at her quick story to put him at his ease.

"Why don't we just sit down and have some coffee, and you can tell me how this...this good news came about and what your plans are and everything."

She dropped into the swivel rocker where she usually sat to watch TV or read. He took the love seat. Her little apartment wasn't large enough to accommodate a full-size sofa. Then she realized she'd offered coffee and hastily jumped up to get it.

"Don't go to a lot of trouble—"

"No trouble." She put water, a filter, and coffee into the coffeemaker, glad to have something to do with her hands. She didn't want him to think she was disturbed about this announcement, didn't want him to think she'd read more into their casual relationship than was there. Because she hadn't, of course. It was just that—

That *what?*

Later, she told herself firmly. Later she'd sort out her feelings. For now it was important to be casual about this. Very casual. And pleasant. Genial. Encouraging. Congratulatory. The list of all the things she should be glowed like neon signs in her head, but underneath lurked a bundle of totally different, very dismaying feelings.

She returned to the chair, hands clasped in her lap. With determined cheerfulness she said, "So, you finally realized you'd made a mistake and decided to get in touch with her?"

"Well, no. Perhaps you remember my mentioning that she has an elderly aunt, a great-aunt, actually, who lives here in Seattle?"

Silver nodded. "Yes, I remember."

"Last week Aunt Louise fell and shattered her hip. Silver came up, of course, and we've both spent a lot of time at the hospital with her aunt over the past week. For a while it looked as if Aunt Louise might not make it, but she's much improved now. She was moved to a nursing home and rehabilitation center this morning and will be there for several weeks. After that she'll need home care for a while, but she should make a good recovery eventually. Which is a wonderful blessing for Silver, of course. Except for Tyler, Aunt Louise is the only living relative Silver has."

Hearing her own name spoken in reference to another person felt strange, even a little shivery, Silver thought. Perhaps if you had a common name it was something you became accustomed to, but she still felt, well, odd hearing it. Then she dismissed all that as irrelevant. And foolishly self-centered, too. She concentrated on making her expression bright and attentive as Chris went on.

"So, after being together so much during the last week, we just finally got around to talking about our relationship, and we decided to give it another chance. I remember your telling me that I'd broken up with her rather arbitrarily, without even trying to work things out, and I decided you were right and I probably had been unfair."

"Have you made definite plans, then?" She swallowed. "Marriage—?"

"No. We've just decided to give it another try and see what happens. Silver is going back to Portland in the morning because of her crafts shop, but she plans to spend every weekend here until Aunt Louise is back on her feet. So we'll have more time together than we've had before. We both decided that in spite of seeing each other more or less regularly over the past year that we really didn't know each other very well. She said the letter I sent her showed her a side of me that she didn't even know existed. She said she probably wouldn't even have felt she could call me about Aunt Louise if she hadn't received that letter."

"I hope everything works out for the best for you, Chris." Silver could honestly say that even as she felt a bungee-jump plunge of emotion deep inside. "You're a pretty special kind of guy."

"Thanks. And thanks for being so…sweet and generous and understanding about everything. I'm not much good at flowery speeches of appreciation, but knowing you has been a real blessing from the Lord."

Silver felt an unwanted gathering of tears, and she quickly cut off the flow with a tart remark. "Then you won't mind my giving you one more piece of advice. I doubt the Lord considers how many motels a person owns as particularly important in his eternal scheme of things."

Chris blinked as if she'd sneaked up on him with that zinger. "Well, I'm sure that's true, but—"

"Silver and Tyler can't be shoved into the background while you play corporate takeover games. At least not if you want a happy, lasting relationship."

Chris's faint scowl relaxed into a grin. "Okay, Counselor, I'll remember that. Would you also like to offer a little credit-counseling advice on my current financing problems?" he teased gently. "The bank is not exactly wholeheartedly behind me yet."

"Sorry. My expertise has a credit limit in the thousands, and I rather think you're well above that."

He turned his head slightly, and some trick of the lamplight suddenly highlighted that thin white scar on his temple. For a moment she was tempted to ask bluntly how he'd gotten it. She'd always been curious, and now she'd never see him again and would never know.

She squelched the impulse and stood up, not necessarily

trying to hurry him out, but wanting him to go before her mixed emotions betrayed her. Their bantering had helped her get herself under control, but she might still dissolve into tears if she wasn't careful. Although, she didn't know why the tears lurked there. This was certainly no heartbreaking disaster. It wasn't as if she'd been picking out a wedding gown or naming their children; they'd simply had a few fun times together. "Thanks for coming in person to tell me this."

He stood up, too. "See how I've improved under your tutelage?" he teased lightly. "Just call me Mr. Sensitive in Seattle."

"I don't know that I'd go *that* far."

"There's just one more thing."

"Yes?" she said warily.

"I told Silver, the other Silver, about meeting you and about the peculiarity of your names being exactly the same. She'd like to meet you."

"Meet me?" Silver repeated in surprise and dismay. "Why?"

"I don't know. Curiosity, I suppose. Because she was as astonished as you were to hear about someone else with the same unusual name."

Or maybe to check me out as a defeated rival? But Silver instantly discarded that snide thought. They weren't rivals. She and Chris had never had anything more than a friendly and casual relationship, which was exactly what he had probably told the other Silver.

"Look, I know it would be rather awkward." Chris sounded apologetic. "I don't think much of the idea myself."

Silver hesitated, thoughts flying and colliding. She didn't want to meet this other Silver, the one Chris had chosen over her! Well, no, that wasn't quite true. She'd always been curious about this other Silver, in a way that had nothing to do with Chris. How could she *not* be curious about someone with the very same name she had? Was there any similarity between them? Did they think alike, look alike, act alike? But in spite of the curiosity, the idea of meeting "the other woman" made her skin prickle with a definite queasiness. What could they possibly have to say to each other? Yet if she refused to meet the other Silver, it might look as if she truly had thought there was something romantic between herself and Chris, a thought he'd apparently never had.

Sensing her indecision, Chris said hastily, "You don't have to decide now. I can give you a call when she's here this weekend and see what you've decided. And don't think you have to do it. We can just forget the whole thing. As I said, I don't think it's such a great idea myself."

His repetition of that statement suddenly made her curious. "Why not?"

He shifted uncomfortably on his feet. "It just sounds, well, awkward."

"Are you afraid we're going to stage a hair-pulling, fingernail-clawing catfight over you?" She suppressed a smile at the incongruous mental image.

"Don't be ridiculous," he scoffed, straightening as if he were a cornered cat arching its back. "Of course not."

But a certain giveaway color to his face—a blush! Chris Bentley was blushing!—told her he actually had worries about what might happen at a meeting. She was momentarily indignant. How could he possibly think she'd do something outrageous and embarrassing? On second thought, however, given his memories of a certain scene in an espresso shop, his apprehension was perhaps understandable.

"I assure you, I'll be on my very best behavior," she said with all the shoulder-squared dignity she could muster. "As I'm sure the other Silver will be also."

Which at that point, she realized with a certain dismay, said that she'd committed herself to this meeting even though she hadn't actually decided she wanted to do it.

"Well, okay, then. I'll give you a call when she comes up this weekend, and we'll set something up." He lifted his arm and looked at his watch. "I'd better get going. I'm meeting Silver and Tyler for dinner in a few minutes. So I'll talk to you later about this."

"Tell her I'm looking forward to the meeting."

Which was stretching the truth, she had to admit after Chris was gone. But she was curious. She also realized that she'd never gotten around to serving the coffee, and the spaghetti sauce was cold. And she seemed to have lost her appetite.

After staring absently at the coffeemaker for a full minute, she finally poured a cup and carried it to the swivel rocker. She looked at the empty love seat. The throw pillow still bore a slight indentation where Chris's hip had rested against it.

She wasn't really upset about this, she assured herself, as she sat there clutching the hot coffee cup with both hands. It wasn't the breakup of some big romance, not the crushing blow it had been when Brad tossed her his *arrivederci*. Maybe her heart was a tiny bit more involved with Chris than she'd allowed herself to acknowledge, but she certainly wasn't in love with him.

Although she wasn't all that far from it.

For a while, even though she had scoffed at the idea with Colleen, she had toyed with the possibility that Chris was perhaps the man the Lord had in mind for her. The unlikely way they'd met, the tickets to Reba McEntire…all the unlikely incidents that seemed as if they could have been engineered by God.

But perhaps her perspective had been skewed. Perhaps it wasn't a love relationship between her and Chris that the Lord had in mind; perhaps her place in the Lord's scheme of things had simply been as a tool, an instrument, to help Chris and the other Silver find their way back together.

And if that was true, it was not for her to protest or question the Lord's will or decision. She swallowed, hard, forcing down the peculiar lump in her throat. She should simply be glad that the Lord had found her a useful instrument in working out his will. Though she was poised right on the brink of falling in love with Chris, she should be glad she hadn't actually plunged into love for a man God intended for another woman.

It was a thought she clung to and repeated to herself frequently as the days went by. She also clung to a hope that the other Silver would forget about wanting to meet her, that the whole idea would somehow simply fizzle into irrelevance. Or perhaps she'd be busy when Chris called, and she could honestly excuse herself on that basis.

It didn't work that way. The other Silver didn't forget, and her own weekend was as empty as a desert island a thousand miles from nowhere when Chris called.

And reluctantly she heard herself saying with feigned delight, "Yes, of course I'd love to drop by for coffee with you and Silver on Saturday afternoon."

Eleven

 ilver rang the doorbell on the neat, sunny yellow house, then surreptitiously dried her damp palm on the tissue in her pocket. Was she underdressed in her tailored blue pants and white sweater for afternoon coffee with the other Silver and Chris? Maybe she should have gone for the gold with something knockout sophisticated. Not that she owned anything that was actually in the knockout sophisticated category.

She was at a certain disadvantage here, meeting the other Silver on her home territory, she thought uneasily. Perhaps she should have insisted on some neutral meeting place.

Ridiculous. This wasn't, after all, some claws-bared contest. She and the other Silver were meeting simply because they were both curious about someone else with the same name. So, if nothing else, they obviously shared this mutual trait of curiosity.

The door opened, and the two women stared at each other. The other Silver—though for a brief moment Silver saw that from the perspective of the petite, dark-haired woman standing in the doorway, *she* was the other Silver—hesitated only a moment before smiling.

"Silver Sinclair?" she said.

"*Not* the one and only," Silver responded, and both women laughed.

"Come in."

A fragrance of freshly baked cookies met Silver when she stepped inside. A little boy raced down from upstairs but stopped short when he saw her, obviously disappointed that she wasn't someone else. That gave Silver an uneasy clue that Chris wasn't here yet. That made him definitely late, because she was late herself, having had some difficulty finding the address in the unfamiliar neighborhood.

"Tyler, come down and meet a new friend," the other Silver called to the boy.

As he approached and his mother introduced them, Silver could see why Chris was so taken by the little boy. Tyler was dark blond and wiry, proudly wearing an oversized Sonics T-shirt, no doubt a gift from Chris. He offered his hand for a dignified, man-of-the-house handshake, but his hazel eyes bubbled with energy and mischief. He didn't seem to find anything unusual about this new woman having the same name as his mother.

"What are you doing upstairs?" his mother asked.

"Nothin'." he answered with adorable, if somewhat suspicious, innocence and a definitely suspicious squirm.

"Just make certain 'nothin' doesn't include getting into the train set until Chris gets here." To Silver she added, "My uncle had this old, broken-down train set, and Chris got it running for Tyler. But, on his own, if Chris isn't here to oversee, Tyler tends to send all the cars crashing into wild train wrecks."

Tyler grinned guilty agreement, and his mother gave him a cookie and scooted him off to play with his trucks in another room. The two women looked at each other again. The first minutes of their meeting hadn't made any hazardous waves, but now what? Oh, this could definitely be very awkward, Silver thought with a rising panic. What were they going to do? Discuss the weather? Compare notes on Chris? Continue to just stand here appraising each other?

The other woman was a few years older. Her dark hair curled softly around her heart-shaped face and beautiful brown eyes; she radiated a gentle, appealing femininity, someone who never lost her temper, someone whose cookies never burned and whose house never looked like a sanctuary for refugee dust balls. Silver felt too large, bones too prominent and knobby, as if she couldn't move without sending furniture crashing in all directions. And why, why, hadn't she done something different with her hair? Next to the other Silver's soft, dark cloud, her wild spiral perm felt like a mad hairdresser's experiment gone awry. Obviously, as far as physical attributes went, they couldn't be more different.

"Won't you sit down?" The other Silver motioned her to a brown sofa in the living room, beside which was an old-fashioned fringed floor lamp. The carpet was also old-fashioned, a dark, twisting floral. "Would you like coffee now, or shall we wait for Chris?"

"Wait, I guess." Silver perched uneasily on the edge of the sofa, feeling as she had in high school when she was up against the state champion in the one-hundred-meter dash. She definitely hadn't counted on this, being trapped here alone with the other Silver. Where *was* Chris?

The other woman smiled, apparently sensing Silver's discomfort. She looked small and delicately graceful in the big overstuffed chair. "I'll ask you the question I've been asked so many times. How did you happen to get our unusual name, Silver?"

It was a logical question. That was what this meeting was about, their identical names. Silver was grateful the other woman had taken the initiative, and she rushed into explanation. "I think that was the first question I asked my parents when I learned to talk, because by then I'd already heard, 'What an odd name,' about a thousand times. My mother said they named me that because when I was born I had this whole mane of fantastic, silvery blond hair, and everyone just oohed and aahed over it." Silver wrinkled her nose and stretched out a long, corkscrew-curled strand to look sideways at it. "Of course, now, when I could use something spectacular, it's turned into this wouldn't-you-like-to-try-some-bleach-on-that blond."

"It's a wonderful color, and don't let anyone try to tell you it isn't," the other Silver said with an unexpected emphasis that sounded sincere. "And those wild, carefree-looking spiral curls are fantastic on you."

"So how did you get the name?" Silver asked curiously.

The other Silver shook her head. "I don't know. I wish I did. My parents were killed when I was four. I was raised in several different foster homes. This was before Aunt Louise and I located each other." She smiled lightly. "My parents were flower-children types of the late sixties, so I was probably lucky I wasn't named something even stranger. I could have been Lovebeam or Moonflower or something."

"I guess there are worse names than Silver," Silver agreed. "Actually, I rather like it now."

"I do, too. It isn't something you hear every day. Present company excepted, of course." They smiled at each other with a small sense of camaraderie.

Curiously Silver asked, "Was it someone in a foster home who led you to the Lord?"

"No. I was never fortunate enough to encounter that kind of foster home." She didn't elaborate, but she spoke without bitterness or accusation. Still, Silver got the definite impression that the other Silver's early years were definitely not the life of which happy childhood memories are made. And then to lose her husband, too. Thinking of her own loving family and secure childhood, her heart unexpectedly wrenched for this woman whose life had been so much harder, marveling at how little it had affected her gentle face and warm smile. A peace and acceptance that could only have come from the Lord, Silver knew.

"I didn't become a Christian until after I met my husband," the other Silver explained. "From whom I also got the Sinclair name that makes our names identical. Before that I was Silver Parker." She stood up suddenly. "How about some coffee and cookies? I don't see any point waiting any longer for Chris. Come on out to the kitchen with me."

Silver followed her to the kitchen, pleasantly old-fashioned with tall, white cabinets decorated with floral decals. The other Silver poured coffee in a delicate china cup decorated with twined roses. The cookies were a simple peanut-butter type, but they were perfectly shaped, perfectly marked with even lines, perfectly unburned.

"I understand you have a crafts store down in Portland?"

"Yes. We specialize in handling all types of doll-making materials and supplies. I also teach an occasional class in doll making." She smiled. "Somehow I suspect you are not wildly interested in doll making."

Silver lifted a shoulder in a rueful semishrug. "Not really. I'm more the athletic type."

"I like to watch figure skating and gymnastics on TV." The other Silver sounded hopeful, and Silver shook her head regretfully.

"I've always been more interested in the speed events." Finally she impulsively stated the obvious. "We're not much alike, are we, except for our names."

"Middle names! What's yours?"

"Anne. After my grandmother," Silver answered. "What's yours?"

"Sequoia. Silver Sequoia." She laughed ruefully. "I told you my parents were sixties flower children. And, to answer your question, I guess we're not really much alike." She also sounded regretful.

Silver looked at her watch. "I wonder where in the world Chris is? I really should be going."

"He called just before you arrived and said he'd be a little late."

"He's probably tied up on something concerning that big business deal with the other motel chain."

"Probably," the other Silver agreed. Then her smooth brow unexpectedly wrinkled. "Unless he's just plain chicken."

Silver blinked, astonished at the unexpected word coming from this sweetly demure lady. "Chicken?" she repeated doubtfully.

"I'm not sure what he's been worried would happen when you and I met. But he's definitely been worried." The other Silver shook her cloud of dark hair with her own definite hint of annoyance. "I'm wondering now if he isn't just hiding out somewhere, dragging his feet about showing up because—"

"Because he's chicken!" Silver filled in gleefully, delighted with this unexpected meeting of minds. "I suggested to him, when he kept repeating that I didn't have to meet you, that he was afraid we'd get into some jealous, hair-pulling, screaming, clawing fight if we got together." No, she hadn't included the word *jealous* to Chris, but it had hung unspoken between them.

"Oh, did you really?" The other Silver clapped her hands. "That's marvelous! I love it. Maybe we should put on a little show for him when he arrives!"

Even though Silver knew the other woman wasn't serious,

the idea held a frivolous appeal. "He'd panic, wouldn't he? The Mighty Motel Mogul frantically trying to figure out how to separate us!"

The other Silver laughed, a heartier laugh than Silver would have expected out of one so delicate looking. "Actually, it wasn't until after this was all scheduled that I realized you and Chris had had more than an accidental meeting, that you'd actually been dating. Until then, it hadn't occurred to me that this could be, well…a little awkward."

"Oh, but we haven't really been *dating,*" Silver denied quickly. "We just went skiing and bike riding a time or two. There was nothing romantic involved, nothing romantic at all!"

The other Silver squeezed her arm reassuringly. "It's fine. I went out with a guy down in Portland a few times myself. And whatever you've done to Chris seems to have done him a world of good. He tries so hard to be thoughtful now. So, when you were in grade school, did the kids drive you crazy making fun of your name, the way they did me?"

The abrupt change of subject momentarily startled Silver. She just stood there, cookie poised halfway to her mouth.

"They were rerunning some old Lone Ranger shows on TV, and I heard 'Hi-Yo, Silver, away!' so often from the other kids that I sometimes felt like sending that horse of the Lone Ranger's a package of poisoned sugar lumps," the other Silver declared.

"I did worse than just think about doing something," Silver admitted. "There was one boy who kept making cracks about me being as big and dumb as the Lone Ranger's horse. So one day I backed up to him and kicked him in the shins, just like a horse." She shook her head, remembering the lecture and all the trouble that had gotten her into.

"And sterling, sterling Silver!" the other Silver exclaimed. "Once a teacher left the room, and all the kids except me started running around and throwing things, and when the teacher came back she held me up as an example to everyone, this wonderful girl of sterling character. And everyone hated me for it, of course, and one boy named his dog Sterling Silver and was always talking at school about how Sterling Silver had been rummaging in the garbage or burying bones in the backyard." She rolled her eyes in exasperated memory.

Silver laughed and nodded, unexpectedly delighted with this comparing of notes from the past. People who had ordinary names didn't realize how awful it could be as a child to have an unusual one. "And then there were the people who seemed to think you'd tried to glamorize yourself by calling yourself by some phony, movie-star-sounding name. Although that wasn't as bad as getting Silver shortened to Sil, which then became Silly. And then a miserable cousin of mine made up this dumb rhyme, *Silly Silver's hair's like a wig, dirty and stinky as an ugly old pig.* So I smeared glue all over the back of *his* hair, and his mother had to shave his head to get it off—"

The sudden appearance of Chris in the kitchen doorway startled them both. He looked at the two of them where they sat giggling like girls at a slumber party. "I rang the doorbell, but apparently you two were so busy laughing in here that you didn't even hear it."

"We were just comparing notes," the other Silver said.

Chris's half-dismayed, half-wary look indicated he thought that surely meant they were comparing notes about him. Not very complimentary notes.

Silver didn't let him off easy. "Actually, we were just taking time-out to catch our breath between bouts of clawing and scratching and hair pulling."

"She's the hair-pulling champ, but I'm better at clawing." The other Silver held up her hand and with a mischievous smile flexed her fingers at him, and then the two women looked at each other and grinned conspiratorially.

"Okay, you two, I get the message," Chris growled.

Just then Tyler, with small-boy bluntness, yelled from the bathroom that there was no paper, and the other Silver went to remedy the situation.

"Chris Bentley, I think you halfway wanted us to fight over you," Silver declared. "And now you're disappointed because we're getting along just fine."

"Don't be ridiculous," he muttered. "Although I don't suppose I expected to find the two of you acting as if it were old home week." He hesitated and then asked almost plaintively, "Couldn't you at least have pretended there was a little rivalry here? Exchanged a few catty remarks? I'm beginning to feel like the kid nobody wants on their team. 'You take him,' one side says. 'No, we took him last time; you take him.'"

Silver laughed. "She's a wonderful woman, Chris," she said sincerely. "I'm glad I had a chance to meet her."

The other Silver returned, little Tyler with her. His face lit up when he saw Chris, and like a small, blond cannonball he hurled himself at the man. Chris swept him up in his arms and held him high overhead, and Silver felt a peculiar little lump in her throat at the sight of the obvious affection between them.

"You been causing more train wrecks upstairs?" Chris asked with mock sternness.

"No! I been waitin' for you!" The boy giggled. "Well, maybe one little wreck."

Silver set her coffee cup on the counter. "I should be going. I want to take my bike out for a couple hours yet this afternoon." Specifically to the other Silver she added, "Thanks for the coffee and cookies…and everything."

"It was wonderful meeting you."

At the door, Silver impulsively hugged the other Silver and, after a moment's hesitation, hugged Chris, too. She still had to deal with a certain private, lingering regret that Chris had not been the man the Lord meant for her. But he was in good hands. She was sure of it.

"Hi-Yo, Silver," she said softly to the other woman.

"Hi-Yo, Silver," the other Silver echoed back.

Chris looked bewildered. But both women were smiling.

Twelve

o, that takes care of that, Silver thought as she headed home. Would they invite her to their wedding? Yes, probably. Would she go? Yes. Even different as she and the other Silver were, even while she still felt an unwanted little undercurrent of attraction for Chris herself, she very much liked the other Silver and could sincerely wish them the best.

She did not, however, take that bike ride she had planned for the remainder of the afternoon. To her surprise, a woman jumped out of a battered old Honda and ran toward her as soon as she pulled into her parking spot at the apartment complex. Silver rolled down the window.

"Karyn!" she exclaimed. She hadn't heard from the young mother with so many problems recently, and hadn't been able to reach her when she tried to call.

"I'm so sorry to bother you at home, but your office is closed, and I just didn't know what else to do. I've been evicted from my apartment!" In disconnected, jerky gasps Karyn explained how a dental emergency with infected wisdom teeth had disrupted the debt-repayment plan and budget Silver had worked out for her. And how she had so far fought off the attempts of her husband's parents to get her children, but without a place to live they might now succeed. The two children watched big-eyed and solemn from the car.

There were temporary shelters, of course, to which Silver could have referred Karyn, but she didn't hesitate to offer an alternative that involved herself personally. "You can stay here with me until we figure out something."

"I couldn't—"

"Yes, you can," Silver said firmly. She'd have to do some fast talking to the apartment manager and pay extra rent, but she'd manage it.

Together Silver and Karyn carried necessities from the heavily loaded car up to the apartment. Silver gave them the bedroom. She had an air mattress she used for camping trips that she could spread on the living-room floor for her own use.

They couldn't do much about finding financial help for Karyn on the weekend, but Silver got their temporary stay in the apartment okayed with the manager. While the girls played at the apartment complex's small playground, she and Karyn discussed possible solutions to the problems. That night they prayed together and all went to Sunday school and church together the following morning.

She talked to the pastor about the problem later that day, discussed it with Colleen on Monday, and made numerous phone calls, but all she could come up with was temporary assistance. Which was welcome, of course, but the little family needed more. Landlords wanted first and last months' rent plus a hefty security deposit; government rental assistance meant getting on a list and waiting. They again presented the problem in prayer to the Lord that evening, and Silver was pleased with how open, even hungry, Karyn was for spiritual help and guidance.

But by the following Monday, the problem of a more permanent place for Karyn and her children to live was still unsolved. One thing the situation did, however, was effectively keep Silver's mind off Chris. With Karyn and the two lively girls in residence, she was surrounded by too much noise and energy and activity for dabbling in troublesome personal matters.

A new problem, however, in the form of the office manager, Mr. Landeau, soon jumped up to confront her. He came to her cubicle and said he'd heard rumors that she had a client living in her home.

"We cannot, you understand, try to force our own personal beliefs on clients."

Silver just stared at him, astonished at this interpretation of her efforts to help Karyn, before protesting, "I'm not forcing anything."

"You have, have you not, taken this client to your church? Given her instruction in your own personal religious views? And your help was given to her on the condition she cooperate with your indoctrination? Whether stated or unstated, your conditions are obvious."

Mr. Landeau's accusations so twisted the help Silver was trying to give Karyn—indoctrination!—that she hardly knew where to begin a vehement protest. "She's a guest in my home, not a...a religious conquest!"

"Nevertheless, this sets a dangerous precedent."

Everyone was well aware that Mr. Landeau interpreted various rules considerably more rigidly and narrowly than the former manager had done. In the office, each counselor had strict limits on how much time could be devoted to any one client. Making small talk to set a nervous client at ease was now classified as inefficiency, and nothing less than a near-death collision on the freeway was an acceptable excuse for lateness. It was also well known that Mr. Landeau had only a poorly veiled scorn for people with active religious beliefs. But Silver was still astonished by this.

"You can't tell me what to do on my own time, in my own home! That's a violation of…something." She was furious that her ending came out as more of a sputter than a word, and a weak word at that. She was certain Mr. Landeau couldn't tell her what to do after hours, but she wasn't quite sure on what legal basis. "And if you do try to…restrict what I do, I will file a formal complaint!" She also wasn't certain with whom she'd file it, but she'd find someone!

Mr. Landeau's eyes, "beady little eyes," as Colleen called them, narrowed, but the threat of a complaint apparently made him back off. "I am merely trying to protect this office from any accusations of religious bias with clients," he said with stiff self-righteousness before turning on his heel and leaving Silver silently fuming.

Mr. Landeau said nothing further during the following week, but Silver knew he was watching her, no doubt hoping to nail her for some infraction here in the office since she hadn't meekly given in to his complaint about Karyn. Before, she had occasionally suggested a Christian counseling center when she could see a family had more than financial difficulties, but now she felt constrained about offering even that minimal spiritual assistance.

After Karyn and the girls had been in her apartment almost three weeks, Karyn herself came up with a surprise idea. "It came to me in bed last night, after we prayed. I think…maybe it came from the Lord," she offered tentatively. She shook her head. "But it sounds so dangerous."

Silver listened to the idea, and despite some apprehensions, on Saturday they acted on it, joining hands for another prayer before walking up to ring the doorbell on the large, older home in Kirkland, on the east side of Lake Washington where Silver and Chris had biked in the rain. As they stood there waiting for someone to come to the door, she could think of him without that lingering, faintly regretful, what-might-have-been feeling. Well, almost without it, she amended slightly, with an inner sigh.

She could also think, as Karyn had mentioned, that what they were doing here was indeed dangerous, like Christians strolling unarmed into the lions' den. Karyn's in-laws, who had been trying to get custody of the girls, might reach out of the "den" and snatch them.

When the door opened, the middle-aged woman and Karyn just eyed each other warily for a tense moment. Then the girls chorused, "Grandma!" and Silver saw the troubled look in the eyes of the woman in the doorway melt. She shook her head in an oddly helpless way.

"Karyn, we thought we were doing the right thing, going to the lawyer about custody," the woman said softly, "but I've been feeling worse and worse about it."

Within a half hour it was arranged. Not a custody change but a family arrangement that benefited everyone. Karyn and the girls would live right here with her in-laws. The Andersons would know their grandchildren were cared for and safe; Mrs. Anderson could even take care of them while Karyn worked. They would all be cooperating together for the good of the children, not uselessly battling each other from behind the shields of lawyers.

"Why didn't I think of this?" Silver marveled as they returned to her apartment to pick up Karyn's and the girls' belongings.

"I don't think it would have worked this way earlier. Maybe because the Lord wanted to show me what he could do," Karyn offered a little shyly. "I think it took him to soften the Andersons' hearts." She smiled. "And mine."

Silver appreciated having her own bed back after Karyn and the girls were gone. She appreciated being able to get in the bathroom whenever she wanted. A friend contacted her about a phone campaign in protest of a series of suggestive advertisements on a local radio station, and she kept busy on that for several evenings. But she almost hated to return to the apartment at night, knowing how silent and empty it would be without Karyn and the girls.

Then she received an unexpected phone call. The other Silver sounded hurried and agitated. And her request—could she come over and talk to Silver for a few minutes?—surprised and alarmed her.

Thirteen

The other Silver arrived as Silver was putting her dinner leftovers in the refrigerator. She'd found it hard to go back to cooking for just one after having Karyn and the girls' healthy appetites with her for three weeks. The other Silver noticed her peering around, obviously looking for Tyler.

"I left him with a neighbor of Aunt Louise's," she explained. "I wanted to talk to you alone. He's going to be so upset…"

"Is it Chris?" Silver asked gently. "Don't tell me his business has gotten in the way again."

"Oh, no! He's been wonderful. Making such an effort to be sweet and thoughtful." She tilted her head to one side and smiled. "In his own rather preoccupied way, of course."

Silver took the white jacket that set off the other Silver's dark hair so nicely and hung it in the closet. "This sounds as if it requires a serious cup of coffee."

"Could I impose on you to make that tea?"

Silver wasn't much of a tea drinker, but she found some old tea bags in the cupboard, made a cup for the other Silver, and poured coffee for herself. They settled in the living room, the other Silver perching on the love seat where Chris had sat a few weeks ago when he told Silver they were getting back together.

"As you may know," the other Silver began, "I was the one who suggested that Chris and I make another try at our relationship." She lifted dark eyebrows questioningly to confirm that Silver knew this.

"Well, uh, no, I didn't know that." It didn't change anything, of course, and yet Silver felt as if she were peering around a different corner at the situation. But the fact that Chris hadn't mentioned this detail wasn't surprising, of course. He still might not win any gold stars in the sensitivity department, but he was definitely a gentleman about privacy matters.

"I thought, when we broke up earlier, that it was the right thing to do. But he was so wonderfully helpful with Aunt Louise, and it felt so good to be able to turn to him for advice and encouragement and strength, so comforting to lean on him again, and Tyler is so crazy about him."

"Yes, I could see that when I was at your aunt's. And I know Chris feels the same way about Tyler."

"That's part of what makes this so difficult." She put her cup of tea on the coffee table and laced her fingers together. "Because I want out."

"Out?"

"Out," the other Silver repeated with greater emphasis. "Chris really is a wonderful guy in so many ways. A godly man, a strong man, wonderful with Tyler. But he and I—" She shook her head. "It just isn't working. Name any given subject, and we're on opposite sides of it."

"Not as believers!"

"No. I don't mean that. I mean like the mundane things you have to live with every day. Such as food. We're both into healthful eating, but I like delicate flavors, subtly flavored sauces, light desserts. Chris likes robust flavors, spices hot enough to make my hair stand on end, hearty desserts. I like delicate herbal teas; he likes coffee strong enough to dissolve silverware. Then there's our difference in temperature preferences. I like warm, cozy rooms. He's always flinging windows open and turning the thermostat down. So either he's too hot, and I'm too cold, or the other way around."

"These aren't earth-shattering differences," Silver protested.

"There's more. He loves riding on that monster of a motorcycle; I'd rather walk barefoot over broken glass than get on that thing again. I like a quiet game of chess; he'd rather get out and slam a ball, any ball, around. He likes to climb mountains; I prefer the elevator up the Space Needle. He likes camping out; a tent makes me claustrophobic. My idea of boating is rowing around a calm lake; his is flinging himself down a whitewater river in a raft. He was so helpful in getting my crafts store started, but deep down I think he sees the whole idea of making dolls as basically frivolous. When we were seeing each other only once or twice a month, we sidestepped or glossed over these differences. But I've been staying here in Seattle even more than I originally planned, and we've been together considerably more."

She smiled ruefully. "Would you believe that in all this time I've never even told him I play the harp? Because I realized that if he did know he'd feel obliged to listen to me play, and I also knew he'd be glassy-eyed with boredom."

Silver didn't know what to say. Individually, each item didn't sound of great importance. But added together they almost screamed incompatibility.

"As you said, Chris is a strong believer. He's wonderfully generous to his church and numerous worthwhile humanitarian causes. But he doesn't give much of *himself*." The dark-haired Silver hesitated and then added almost reluctantly, "And sometimes I'm afraid his ambitions for worldly success take precedence over his relationship with the Lord. He gets so pre-occupied with his expansion and improvement deals that he hasn't time for much of anything else. Including personal relationships."

True, Silver reflected. She'd seen that when he'd canceled plans with her. She'd also seen that he didn't seem to be particularly involved in church affairs and activities. "But that's only because he's tied up in this big deal at the moment," she argued.

The other Silver shook her head. "Then there'll be another big deal. And another after that. Sometimes he just seems… driven."

Silver twisted the cup in her hands, the coffee sliding around the rim in dark tidal waves. Yes. *Driven.* It was an appropriate word. "But driven by what?" She felt vaguely bewildered. "He doesn't seem especially interested in luxuries and fancy possessions and material things. He has his condo, of course, and I suppose it was rather expensive. By my standards, that motorcycle also cost a bundle. But he doesn't care about impressing people with some huge, exclusive estate or driving a Ferrari or wearing expensive clothes and jewelry. I doubt that watch he wears cost any more than mine. He's no social climber, and he doesn't seem to be on some power trip." Yet she wasn't really arguing with the other Silver now, just stating the puzzling facts.

"I know. But that doesn't mean he isn't driven toward some goal that is apparently always just out of his grasp."

"Chris told me once that his relationship with you and Tyler had changed his whole outlook on life. That it had made him see what he was missing without a wife and family in his life."

"Maybe so. But it hasn't changed how he actually runs his life. Even now, when I know he's trying to make things work between us, he's still a workaholic."

Silver well remembered that she'd used exactly that word with him. "Did you ever ask him why it was so important to him to have all these more and bigger and better motels?"

"Yes, I did. But whatever the reason is, he wasn't willing to share it with me. He just kind of talked around it." She paused. "Which is perhaps far more significant than anything I've already mentioned. If he can't share something that is so vitally important to him with me, then we're…missing something."

Impulsively Silver asked a totally unrelated question. "Did he ever tell you how he got that scar on his temple?"

The other Silver shook her head negatively. "I've always had the impression that it came from something tragic or violent in his past, that it wasn't just the result of some childish accident or escapade. But he isn't inclined to talk about it, and I never really felt close enough to him to ask. Which also says something about the shortcomings of our relationship, doesn't it?"

The two women sat in reflective silence for long minute until Silver finally asked tentatively, "And you are telling me all this because—"

"Because I was the one who pushed for a reconciliation; I was the one who argued that we should make a second try. And Chris has been trying, and he's so attached to Tyler. So how do I now tell him that I want out?"

"Are you really, totally, completely, honestly sure you do want out?"

"Yes. I'm not sorry we tried again. I had many nagging doubts the first time. I don't now. I'll always care about Chris. I wish him the best. But marriage? No." The final word was almost fervent.

Hesitantly, feeling she was perhaps prying into personal details, Silver asked, "Has he asked you to marry him?"

"No. But that's what this second try was all about, of course. I'm just sorry, for Tyler's sake, that we couldn't make it work."

"Yes. A boy needs a father."

The other Silver smiled lightly. "I suppose I shouldn't have bothered you with all this, but from what Chris said, your abilities as a counselor cover more than credit problems."

"I don't think you really came to me for advice or counseling," Silver said gently. "You know what you have to do."

"Yes." The rise and fall of the dark-haired Silver's chest was more sigh than breath. "Just tell him all this, the same as I've told you. Because what I really needed was just someone sympathetic to talk to, so I could put it all into words and get it straight in my own head."

"Yes."

"And you've been that person." The other Silver stood up. She smiled. "I think I can do it now. Thanks, Silver."

"You're welcome, Silver."

The oddity of calling each other by the same name suddenly struck them both as humorous, and impulsively they shared a warm good-bye hug. Silver retrieved the other woman's jacket from the closet.

"I hope it all works out right for both of you, whatever *right* is in this situation," Silver said sincerely.

"I'll let you know," the other Silver promised.

She called two days later. She sounded, if not quite bubbly, at least buoyant with relief.

"It was the oddest thing. Chris came over for dinner. After he read Tyler a story and tucked him into bed, we were just sitting there, me drinking my herbal tea and Chris his acid-strength coffee, and there was this awkward silence. Then we both started to say something, and when we sorted it out, what we were both saying was that there was something we had to talk about."

"He had come to the same decision you had?"

"Yes! And it was…well, not wonderful, but okay. I cried a little, and he almost did. But we prayed together, and we hugged, and it's all over. No hard feelings. Just…relief, for us both, I think. I'll break it to Tyler a little at a time, so he gradually gets used to the idea. We're going to be okay."

"I'll be praying for you."

"Thanks, Silver. Thanks for everything."

Silver hung up the phone and stared off into space. And how, she wondered uncertainly, did *she* feel about the outcome of all this?

Fourteen

ilver requested her vacation time for the middle two weeks in August, putting the application in early to be sure she'd get the weeks she wanted. She'd spend the first week as a girls' tent counselor at the church's summer camp and decide later what to do with the second week.

She and Colleen conducted a group credit-counseling session one evening for a local civic group. Mr. Landeau unexpectedly dropped in on it. He said he was simply initiating a new evaluation procedure, but Silver suspected he was spying to see if they were "indoctrinating" the group. She substituted in the church nursery one Sunday while the regular woman was away, and started working out on a new machine at her health club. She had a nice letter from the other Silver saying that a family with a little boy Tyler's age had moved in next door, which was helping him with this second-time adjustment to losing Chris, and that she'd started a new doll-making class.

She didn't hear from Chris. And there was no reason she should hear from him, she reminded herself. She wasn't even certain she wanted to hear from him.

Yet when she picked up the phone two weeks later and heard his voice, she felt strangely giddy and light, as if she might float right up to the ceiling. She hastily anchored herself with a grip of bare toes curled into the carpet and managed to murmur, "Hi. How are you?"

Chris, never one for time-wasting small talk, got right to the point. "Would you be interested in a hike on Saturday? The trail up Mount Si should be open now. There's a spectacular view from the top."

Silver filled in with, "Let's see, that's out past Snoqualmie Falls, isn't it?" while she considered both the invitation and the odd—defensive? challenging?—tone in which it was given. Did he feel uncomfortable calling her after trying again with the other Silver? Did she feel uncomfortable about that? If she wanted to be spiteful, she could take the indignant attitude that he'd dropped her like a boring book and who did he think he was now, acting as if he could just waltz in and pick up where they'd left off?

If he noticed her delaying tactic, he didn't comment. "The mountain is a little over four thousand feet, and it's about an eight-mile round-trip hike. Not too strenuous."

Silver could almost hear the other Silver saying with a smile: *Be careful. With Chris, anything that isn't straight up and down is 'not too strenuous.'* Perhaps Chris also heard the other woman saying something because he added, "You do know that the other Silver and I decided we couldn't make it work after all, don't you?"

"Yes, she told me. I'm sorry, Chris. I know the whole situation was difficult for both of you. And Tyler."

"I'm glad we tried again, even if it didn't work," he said, his words paralleling the other Silver's. "It wrapped up all the loose ends. And this time ending it was something we talked about and agreed on together. But, at this point, *you* probably have a right to tell me to go jump in the lake."

"No, I don't feel that way." Silver could say that with honest sincerity. While the situation might feel a bit sticky, she didn't hold Chris's second try with the other Silver against him. She'd always felt there were "loose ends," and now those dangling strands were neatly cut and tied. "Actually, I'd be delighted to take a hike on Saturday."

"Terrific! Pick you up about seven-fifteen?"

"I'll pack a lunch."

"Lunch is on me this time. Just don't expect homemade cookies. By the way, just in case you're wondering, this *is* a date. Maybe not your standard dinner-and-a-movie date, but definitely a date."

"And this means what?" Silver teased, even as she recognized what it did mean, that they were on a subtly different footing now. "That I get a month's free lodging at one of your motels if you don't show up?"

"I'll be there." He paused. "At least I'm 99 percent sure I'll make it." Another pause. "I'll call if I can't."

"Big deal with the takeover still chugging along?"

"Still chugging," he agreed. "But it should be all signed, sealed, and delivered within the next few weeks. Actually, I already own the shares of one of the family members. By the way, we'll take the Gold Wing, of course, on Saturday."

"Of course."

The trail up Mount Si wound back and forth in a series of snake-bend switchbacks, offering sweeping views in several directions as they climbed ever higher on this exhilarating spring day. About halfway up they wandered around a different-looking area called Snag Flat, where board walkways had been built and interpretive signs about the habitat erected. At the summit, sitting atop a rocky outcropping overlooking the most spectacular view of the day, they ate the submarine sandwiches, brownies, and oranges that he'd picked up at a deli. Picturesque small towns and green fields scattered among irregular patches of forest lay below, the occasional red barn standing out like something from a child's toy farm set. Snow-clad mountains stretched to north and south, Rainier and Baker standing out in majestic grandeur.

"I've always wanted to climb Rainier." Chris eyed the mountain as if he were calculating a path to the top of the serene giant.

"It's a two-day climb and definitely very strenuous, but there are guides who furnish equipment and take small groups up." Silver sat up straighter. "Maybe I'll climb Rainier on the second week of my vacation!"

"Are you serious?"

"Why wouldn't I be serious?"

"I guess I've just never known a woman who would suddenly announce she's going to climb the highest mountain in the state." He grinned. "And what do you plan for the first week of the vacation? A little swim across the English Channel, perhaps?"

"Something a lot more dangerous than Rainier or the English Channel. I'll be tent counselor for six girls at our church's summer camp. Last year I was practically smothered when we heard some strange noises and they all piled on top of me in my sleeping bag. And another night they scared me out of my wits when one of the girls painted her hands with some glow-in-the-dark stuff and waved them around in the middle of the night."

Chris laughed. "Okay, you win. Rainier should be a breeze after six girls in a tent."

She gave him a sideways glance as she stuffed plastic wrap

back in the lunch sack. "You're good with kids, and we're still short a couple of counselors for the boys' tents. The camp is out on one of the San Juan Islands. There's swimming, hiking, lots of food, big campfire at night. This camp is for fourth-graders to sixth-graders, and the kids really are terrific. We had a dozen give their lives to Christ last year. Interested?"

"I'll think about it. But I doubt if I could take a week off work. Integrating the Golden Lighthouse chain into Maraben Inns is going to be a big job."

Driven, the other Silver had said. Silver silently sighed and finished picking up the stray bits of her orange peel.

However, a few days later she had her first middle-of-the-week date with him. On his way out to the construction site at Bothell, he popped into the office and took her to lunch. This was also the first time Colleen had gotten an in-person peek at him, and she was impressed.

"Some very high-octane DNA there," Colleen said, nodding sagely. "And wrapped in a very attractive package, too, the kind that ages well. He'll look terrific in your twenty-fifth wedding-anniversary photo."

"Colleen Merriman, you are impossible! We're just friends."

"That might have been true the last time around," Colleen agreed. "But it's a whole new ball game now."

Chris was tied up with business matters all day the following Saturday, but that evening they went out to dinner and a good amateur production of the musical *Seven Brides for Seven Brothers*. He invited her to attend church with him the next day, where she felt curious stares but a certain reserve, as if people knew and respected Chris but weren't particularly close to him

151

personally. That afternoon they rode their bicycles on the trail out toward Woodinville, detouring for ice-cream cones along the way. Back at her apartment, Silver jazzed up a couple of cans of chili with some extra jalapeño peppers, and they grinned at each other as they almost shot out flames as they ate.

Later, when he draped his forearms over her shoulders at the door and slowly and very thoroughly kissed her goodnight, she was engulfed in a delicious glow of warmth.

Oh, yes, this was indeed a different ball game now!

They spent a Saturday morning wandering around the fascinating stalls of the Pike Place Market down near the waterfront, then drove over to Alki Point and found themselves pulled into an impromptu volleyball game on the beach. They got on the same team, but after the first game, the opposite side yelped that this was unfair, that they were both so good they had to split up and play on opposite sides. Afterward Chris astonished her by saying that if she didn't mind living dangerously, he'd cook dinner for her at his condo that evening.

At what he apparently interpreted as a hesitation on her part, he added, "By living dangerously, I mean my cooking. In case you thought the invitation really was for something...more than dinner."

She hadn't thought that. Actually, she was remembering that she was substituting for one of the Sunday school teachers the following morning and still hadn't studied the lesson. But she appreciated having him state this moral stand so plainly. It was nice to know she could say yes without wondering—as she would with some men—if such an invitation included an intimacy she would not accept. She'd just have to leave early to get home in time to study the lesson, she decided.

As it turned out, however, that wasn't what happened.

She waited in the pickup while Chris went into a market to collect the ingredients for what was taking on the aura of a mystery dinner. She peeked into one of the sacks when he set it down while unlocking the door of the top-floor condo. It merely held ordinary staples most people already had in their kitchen: flour, cooking oil, rice, chili powder, and garlic salt.

"I don't do much cooking," he admitted as he stepped back to let her enter first. Overhead a big skylight made the kitchen bright and airy. "About all I eat at home is breakfast. I usually have a dinner meeting of some kind, so I just don't keep much food around."

"But I'm going to get food cooked by the very hands of the Mighty Motel Mogul," she mused. "I'm honored."

"Served with dessert." With a flourish he brought out a lucious-looking chocolate creation from the market's bakery. He grinned a little ruefully as he added a couple of small bottles. "And, just in case this is a complete fiasco, antacids in your choice of liquid or pills."

As she helped put things away, she realized what an extraordinary event this apparently was. Unlike her own refrigerator, where the light was blocked by numerous cartons she hesitated to investigate for fear of encountering hostile life-forms, the dazzling brilliance of his refrigerator held only a half-gallon of nonfat milk, a banana, and a six-pack of Pepsi. His cupboard had breakfast cereals, vitamins, coffee, sugar, salt and pepper, and a couple cartons of noodle mixes. "And to what," she inquired, "do I owe this very special honor?"

He leaned across the items that had come out of the other sack, a cut-up chicken, plus various vegetables and spices, and kissed her lightly. "I'll just let you figure that out for yourself."

She just stood there, carton of rice poised in one hand, uncertain if both the statement and the grin that accompanied it were teasing or mischievous or mysterious. But the possibilities were breathtaking, and to conceal a wild speculation that unexpectedly tumbled her heart like a raft in white water, she hastily asked, "May I help?"

"You can make the salad while I work on the chicken. But first you might like to take a look at the view." He motioned toward the walls of glass wrapping the living room, and she was glad to escape for a moment.

Spectacular. One wall looked out on the city, the Space Needle, and shimmering Elliott Bay, the water alive with everything from churning ferries to skimming sailboats. The other glass wall faced west to more open water where the islands of Puget Sound floated in a misty haze. A small balcony with a wrought-iron railing extended from one end of the glass, on it a rather forlorn-looking chair and metal table.

"It's incredible!" she called. "How do you keep from spending all your time just standing here and looking at the view?" *Especially when there isn't much to see inside,* she added to herself when she finally turned back to the living room. The furniture wasn't quite garage-sale rejects, but not far from it, at definite odds with the luxurious silver gray carpet and architectural elegance of the condo's cathedral ceilings and the white marble fireplace tucked in a corner between the two walls of glass. The television set perched on a low chest of drawers painted a murky green, no doubt some temporary arrangement that had acquired permanency. And the flowery lampshades looked as if they had fallen into the clutches of some maniacal ruffling machine!

How had Chris acquired something so contrary to his personality? She briefly considered, and rejected, the possibility that the other Silver may have chosen them; the other Silver, well dressed and impeccably groomed, had far better taste than that.

"As soon as I get around to it, I'm going to do something

with this place," Chris said when she returned to the kitchen where he was chopping onions and green peppers. He sounded a bit apologetic, so he was apparently not unaware that his decor could use some fine-tuning. Or, better yet, a major overhaul. Yet she also knew he'd been living here at least a couple of years.

"Which means, to put that into a time frame, as soon as you own all the motels on the West Coast?" she asked lightly, tearing crisp leaves of lettuce for the salad.

"This deal with the Golden Lighthouse chain is it, at least for a good long time. There are other things in life."

He sounded sincere, even fervent, and she was pleased. Perhaps he wasn't as driven to strive for some elusive goal as both she and the other Silver feared. She leaned her elbows on the counter to watch him scoop the chopped vegetables into the rice.

"It's a dish my brother's wife made one time, and it was so good that I asked her for the recipe," he explained. "Which astonished both of us, I think."

"So you've made it into your specialty?"

"Nope. First time I've ever tried it."

"I *am* honored!"

The dish turned out to be chicken and rice cooked in a Mexican sauce so fragrant and tempting that Silver was ready to rip the door off the oven when the tantalizing scents started drifting out. But he dragged another chair out to the balcony, and the delay while dinner cooked gave them a relaxed time to sit and talk. The conversation wasn't particularly revealing or intimate, just the kind of comfortable, everyday talk they didn't often share during their busy physical activities. They laughed about incidents at their offices, discussed Mr. Landeau's hostile attitude, talked about a best-selling Christian novel they'd both read.

The chicken was well worth the wait. Succulent and spicy, falling-off-the-bone tender, with a crowning, offbeat embellishment of stuffed green olives. "And just the right touch of cilantro," Silver proclaimed as she tilted her head back and closed her eyes to savor the marvelous blend of flavors.

"I'm thinking of calling it Bachelor's Surprise. The big surprise, of course, being that it's actually edible." He sounded enormously pleased with his success, and Silver was pleased that this really meant something to him.

They stuffed themselves on Bachelor's Surprise, salad, and the exotic chocolate dessert with a luscious mocha cream filling. Afterward she helped clean up, then glanced at her watch.

"I'll have to be going."

"Already? I was thinking we might sit out on the balcony again."

Silver was tempted, but she shook her head and explained about needing to study the lesson for tomorrow morning.

"What's the lesson on?"

"The subject is forgiveness, and the reference is Ephesians 4:32, but that's as far as I got."

He flung one hand to his forehead in a melodramatic gesture of sudden realization. "You know, I think I might have a Bible right here!" He smiled. "Maybe it even has Ephesians 4:32 in it."

Actually, she could spot three Bibles without even trying: one at the end of the kitchen counter, one on a dining-room windowsill, and one on the dark, carved coffee table that was, if not the ugliest piece of furniture she'd ever seen, certainly a contender.

He dropped to the sofa, picked up the Bible on the coffee table, and flipped to the reference in Ephesians with the expertise of a man in familiar territory. "'Be kind and compassionate to one another, forgiving each other, just as in Christ God forgave you,'" he quoted.

Silver dropped down beside him. "On a personal level, forgiveness can be a difficult concept for kids," she mused. "I had some problems with it. After I gave my heart to Jesus, I could accept that God forgave my sins. After all, he was all-powerful God, capable of such magnificent gestures. But when it came down to little ol' me forgiving someone, like when my brother 'borrowed' and lost my new softball or when my best friend suddenly found a new best friend and snubbed me, I had a very hard time with it."

"Yes, I had problems with forgiving, too." Chris's voice turned unexpectedly somber, as if he were thinking of something far larger than the little wrongs of children, and Silver glanced at him sharply. He was looking off into space, staring beyond the lavender blue evening sky, absentmindedly rubbing that thin white scar on his temple.

"Chris?" she said softly, wonderingly, remembering what the other Silver had once said about some dark or tragic secret in his past.

He swallowed, as if he were resolutely swallowing something that hurt going down, but after a moment the hard line of his mouth relaxed. "But it is possible to forgive even the worst of wrongs against us. Jesus did it on the cross when he said, 'Father, forgive them, for they do not know what they are doing,' and that's what we have to do, too."

They moved outside and watched the rosy glow lingering on Mount Rainier long after evening dusk enveloped the balcony, continuing their discussion about forgiveness, how to bring it to the level of the children's understanding, how to relate it to everyday events in children's lives. Yet if she expected him to make some startling revelation about painful wrongs done him in the past, wrongs he'd managed to forgive, she was wrong. He was silent about himself.

Afterward he took her home and, as usual, climbed the

stairs with her to the second-floor walkway. Under the light at her door they turned to face each other.

"Would you like to come in for another cup of coffee?"

"It's almost midnight. I've already taken up all your study time."

"Chris, I got more out of our discussion, more that I can offer the kids tomorrow, than I ever could have studying here alone. It's wonderful to be with someone who's so…comfortable to be with. Someone who cares about the same things I do and believes God's Word is the place to look for guidance."

They had moved into each others arms as they spoke, a drift that felt as natural as swaying to a dreamy ballad. Lifting her face for his kiss felt natural too, and when the kiss finally ended, they both laughed a little breathlessly. Perhaps because laughter was a safety valve for powerful physical feelings they both wanted to keep under control.

He held her a moment longer, then kissed her lightly on the nose. "By the way, I have a surprise for you next Saturday. Be ready at five o'clock…that's in the morning—"

"What could we possibly do at five in the morning?"

"You'll see." He sounded serenely smug. "You'll like this."

"How do you know?"

"Because, my dear, I know you and your adventurous heart. And don't eat breakfast first."

They had dinner together Thursday evening, but he still wouldn't reveal so much as a clue about the surprise. On Saturday morning, the hour so early and dewy that the day still felt in the process of fresh creation, they crossed the almost trafficless Evergreen Point floating bridge and headed north. Silver wondered if he was taking her to see progress on the new motel or to some interesting place for breakfast, but her speculations were interrupted by the sight of something near an off-ramp. Her indignant gasp was apparently audible.

"What's wrong?"

"Do you see that?"

His gaze followed her pointing finger to a billboard on which a bare-legged woman in high heels was shown bending over so the curve of her minishorts-clad posterior extended over the top of the billboard. Her face, peeking up from the level of her knees, wore a flirty smile, and the square footage of her exposed cleavage suggested a liberal miscalculation in the amount of cherry red material needed to cover her curves.

"What's it advertising?" Chris asked.

"Auto parts! Can you believe that? Auto parts!" The sexy public display would have been bad enough even if a scantily clad and suggestively posed woman had some connection with the goods being advertised, but to use something such as this to sell auto parts! And then to add the outrageously suggestive line: *Check us out! We got the best parts in town!* Silver bounced to her knees in the seat to look back and catch the name of the company on the billboard, then started digging in her purse.

"What are you doing?" Chris sounded mildly apprehensive, as if he thought she might be planning to whip out some hidden weapon and attack the billboard on the spot.

"Looking for something so I can write down the name of the company on the billboard."

"There's a scratch pad in the glove compartment."

She found the paper and scribbled the name. Not that there was much chance she'd forget it! Now Chris's apprehensive expression suggested he thought she might be going to attack the company itself.

"Don't worry. I'm not the violent type, just a persistent letter writer when I see something that makes me angry. I don't mean to get up on my soapbox so early in the morning, but I object to an overdisplay of female flesh being used as a sales tool for carburetors and spark plugs. Although, from what I see on TV and in magazines, this is not a majority opinion."

"The general attitude in advertising seems to be 'sex sells,'" he agreed.

An appalling thought struck her. "Does your company use advertising like that?"

"Oh, no, not us," Chris denied hastily. "We stick to showing nice rooms and good rates. Near the freeway you can check out our billboard that gives the locations of our local motels."

Silver had calmed down by the time he turned onto a side road, although she was still silently composing virulent lines to fire off to the offending company. Her thoughts were suddenly distracted by the appearance of an enormous, multicolored, rumpled length of silken cloth in a nearby field. Her eyes widened as the thing suddenly wiggled to life, then slowly began to billow and rise from the ground.

"It's a hot-air balloon! Are we going up in a balloon? Oh, Chris, I've always wanted to go up in a balloon!"

Just as Chris stopped the pickup near a parked van and trailer, a propane burner inside the balloon went on with a roar, shooting out flames, and the balloon majestically rose to full height. The basket for passengers, which had been lying on its side, slowly turned upright.

Silver was so entranced that she didn't even realize Chris had gotten out of the pickup until he opened her door and bowed.

"Your flying chariot awaits, milady."

They and four other waiting passengers climbed into the deep basket that came almost to Silver's chest. The propane flame roared and shot upward into the balloon again, and this time she could feel the heat on her back. And then they rose, not with the zooming speed of a plane, but slowly and majestically changing from earthbound to skyborne creatures.

At first Silver jumped every time the burner roared and flames shot upward like a spurt of dragon's breath, but gradually she became accustomed to it. She squeezed Chris's arm and brushed her head against his shoulder. "This is wonderful! I love it."

"I knew you would."

"Where will we go?" she asked the pilot.

"I can control our up and down movements with the burner. And I can make the balloon turn, which can have some effect on where it goes." He demonstrated by opening slits in the multicolored fabric looming above them, sending the basket into a lazy swirl, then grinned. He was a handsome, weathered man of fifty or so, obviously enjoying himself even if he'd done this a thousand times. "But mostly it's just a matter of where the wind decides to take us." Or the Creator of the wind, Silver added silently.

They drifted slowly southward, over a mostly agricultural valley, like silent observers from another world, and the sounds from below were surprisingly clear when the burner was off. Silver heard a cow bawling, a woman calling her husband to breakfast, a worker hammering on a rooftop. They could peer into hidden backyards and watch baby ducks on a pond serenely paddling after their mother. They waved at people and received enthusiastic waves in return; once a man yelled, "C'mon down and the wife'll serve you tea and crumpets!" Their shadow drifted with them, a giant teardrop with tiny figures in a hanging basket.

Landing was not the precise event of a plane coming down on a runway. The pilot pointed to an open pasture as a likely spot, but a whimsical puff of wind took them in a different direction. They rose to miss electric lines and a road, then floated over a hillside of dense trees that looked untouched by civilization.

They finally came down in a field of grazing sheep that watched them with only mild curiosity. The van and trailer, which had been following, arrived a few minutes later, and while the pilot and chase crew deflated and rolled up the balloon, the pilot's wife prepared ham and scrambled eggs in the van's mobile kitchen.

"That was perfect, an absolutely perfect surprise," Silver sighed as she snuggled against Chris after they were back in the pickup. "For an encore, how about a hike somewhere?"

"Sil, I'd love to, but I have to meet my lawyer for lunch. I thought the Golden Lighthouse deal would be all wrapped up by now, but there are still a couple of details hanging, and I don't want anything to go wrong at this late date."

"Sure, I understand." She started to say something about his coming over for dinner that evening but abruptly stopped. They weren't at the point of being a couple where it could be assumed they'd naturally do something together on a Saturday night.

Yet his next words almost seemed to assume they were a couple. "I'll give you a call in the middle of the week, as soon as the deal is wrapped up, and we'll have dinner and make plans for something fun next weekend, okay?"

"Oh, Chris, I'm sorry. Actually, I won't be here next weekend."

He glanced at her in surprise. "You won't?"

"I think I mentioned that my family is having a reunion for my parents' thirtieth wedding anniversary in early June. It's this coming weekend."

"Oh, I see." He sounded rather taken aback by her announcement

Did *he* think of the two of them as a couple? Silver wondered with a flutter of heartbeat.

"Actually, I'm also taking Friday off at the office. I'll drive

162

over to Idaho that day, the reunion and anniversary celebration will be Saturday, and then I'll start back after we all go to church together on Sunday. It'll mean getting back rather late Sunday night, but I don't want to miss church with the family. I'd like to stay longer, but Mr. Landeau acted as if I'd asked for his right arm just wanting Friday off."

"You'll be staying at your parents' house?"

"Well, more or less. I'll take my sleeping bag and throw it down outside somewhere. There are always so many of us at these things that we spread out like a bunch of invading ants."

"This is family only?"

"Oh, no. Mom and Dad have all kinds of friends from business and church and various groups they belong to, so there'll be lots of other people there."

A peculiar little silence settled between them, as if he were waiting for her to say something. "That was also a terrific breakfast," she finally offered tentatively.

He glanced at her and scowled. "Did it ever occur to you that I also own a sleeping bag? And this might be an appropriate time to expose your family and me to each other?"

She half-turned in the pickup seat to look at him. "*You* want to come?"

"Well, considering that I seem to be inviting myself, yes."

"Chris, of course I'd love to have you come! Everyone is dying to meet you—" She broke off in embarrassment, realizing she'd just revealed that she'd been babbling to people about him. "I mean, do you really think you could get away?"

"This deal will finish up by midweek at the latest, and I think I deserve some time off. I also think meeting family is important when two people get…involved."

Involved.

"Okay! Yes. I'll tell them you're coming. Oh, Chris, this is wonderful!"

Fifteen

ilver called her parents to let them know Chris was coming to the anniversary celebration and reunion with her. She had mentioned him before, although she hadn't actually "babbled" about him, but she knew this announcement would immediately change their perspective on him. When she was a teenager, her parents had always met her dates, but since being on her own, Brad was the only guy she'd ever taken home and formally introduced to them. Did Chris realize, she wondered, briefly feeling a little sorry for him, that he'd be under the parental magnifying glass as a potential son-in-law all the time he was there?

Was he a potential son-in-law? She could answer that with a positive, definite…maybe! No, she wasn't madly in love yet. But if being in love made you feel as if you could fly, she was definitely sprouting a few wing feathers!

The fact that after work on Tuesday she drove all the way out to the Northgate Mall to buy a new bathing suit was probably also meaningful, although she assured herself that the purchase was simply because her old suit was baggy and weather-beaten.

Certainly it had nothing to do with the fact that this would be the first time Chris saw her in a swimsuit.

On Wednesday evening, after returning from church, she whipped off a letter to the auto-parts company named on the billboard. She controlled her initial urge to blast them with a scathing attack and instead, in reasonable and polite terms, told them why the billboard was objectionable and suggested they use more appropriate advertising.

She and Chris needed to talk about plans for the weekend, but he didn't call, and she didn't want to bother him when she knew he was tied up with last-minute details on closing the deal. Yet when she still hadn't heard from him by Thursday evening, she finally dialed the unlisted home phone number he'd given her. All she got was his answering machine, but about ten-thirty he finally called back. He sounded a little ragged.

"Silver, I'm sorry I haven't been in touch, but it's really been a madhouse this week trying to get this deal settled. I didn't call you earlier because I kept thinking we would get it wrapped up—"

"You mean it isn't settled yet?"

"No. I've been in practically nonstop meetings with the Golden Lighthouse heirs and their representatives all week, but we're still negotiating final details, and I just can't leave now."

"I see."

"I do want to meet your family. I'm eager to meet them. Perhaps later."

Her first unhappy reaction was, *Sure. Maybe the next time they have a thirtieth wedding-anniversary celebration!* But she managed to control the fiery sarcasm and simply say stiffly, "We were all really looking forward to having you there for the family celebration."

A tense silence, and then Chris said in a conciliatory tone,

"Sil, I am sorry about this, but maybe you don't realize just how important it is."

"Yes, I think I realize exactly how important this is to you," she said softly, with a sinking feeling of regret. A woman need never worry about another woman as a rival for Chris's affections; he was morally upright, not a man to stray. But there would always be a powerful rival: his business. She was back to that word the other Silver had used in regard to his ambitions: *driven.*

"Look, if we can wrap this up tomorrow, I'll jump on a plane first thing Saturday morning."

"Do you expect to finish tomorrow?"

A small silence answered that incriminating question. Then he said, "Silver, you can't expect me to simply dump this at the last minute. It's the deal of a lifetime, and it's at an extremely crucial point in the negotiations." He sounded half-angry now, as if she were being totally unfair and unreasonable.

And perhaps she was. She felt oddly deflated now, like that hot-air balloon would be if a giant boot suddenly stomped on it. "Well, thanks for calling. I hope everything works out...for the best for you."

Another small silence, as if he were inspecting that comment for double meanings. Finally he said, "We'll talk when you get back."

She put the phone down softly without responding.

She woke up before dawn and left Seattle well ahead of her original time schedule, and she drove with the radio turned up to teenage boom-box levels in an attempt to drown out troubling thoughts and questions about both Chris and herself. She would not let this ruin the weekend! It was midafternoon when she pulled into the small mining town in northern Idaho where she'd grown up. She felt hot and limp from the long drive across central Washington on an unseasonably warm day, but her spirits lifted when she drove into the rural yard of the comfortable, old-fashioned house, the place she would always consider home.

Camping tents scattered on the lawn, great-aunts sipping iced tea on the front porch, uncles and cousins playing horse-shoes, more cousins stringing up a volleyball net, and kids, kids everywhere! Swinging from a rope tied to a tree limb over the pond that passed as a swimming pool, shrieking as they let go and plunged into the water. Throwing Frisbees, wrestling with Chowder, the collie, chasing the cats. Noise, action, balloons…food! Silver could smell something tantalizing barbecuing even as she got out of the car, and a cousin she hadn't seen in two years dashed up to hug her.

"Sil! Where's this fantastic guy we're supposed to meet?" Trisha peered into the backseat of the car as if Silver might have him stashed there.

So much for keeping secret the fact that a guy was supposed to have come with her and that she had, for all practical purposes, been stood up, Silver thought wryly. For a moment anger and frustration and disappointment threatened to engulf her, but she fought off any giveaway display of those feelings and flashed a saucy grin. "Have my folks been dragging out that imaginary man again to try to convince people I'm not going to be a spinster forever?"

Cousin Trisha groaned and giggled in combination. "Isn't that the truth! At least you have brothers and a sister to produce grandchildren, but in my family there's just me to do it all. Hey, I love your hair like that!" She grabbed Silver's arm companionably, and together they "hi"ed and hugged their way through accumulated relatives and into the house, where Silver's mother and various other relatives were preparing enough food for a wagon train.

"Silver, sweetie, it's so good to see you!" Silver's mother cried. She was about half Silver's size, but her hug was big enough to chase away any lingering gloomy feelings. "Dad will be back in a few minutes. He had to run into the office to take care of an emergency toothache."

More hugs from relatives of assorted shapes, sizes, and ages, including Silver's sister Marcia, and then the inevitable curiosity about the missing man. The irrelevant thought occurred to Silver that she'd spent fifty-nine dollars on a swimsuit that could have been far better spent elsewhere, but she dismissed Chris's absence with a casual, "Oh, he couldn't make it after all." She wasn't glad when one of the kids got bucked off a calf he'd tried to ride in the pasture, but she didn't object to the howling interruption.

Her dad, when he got home, momentarily scowled fiercely when Silver explained that Chris hadn't come—heaven help the man who hurt his daughter's feelings!—but Silver assured him that her feelings were just fine.

All the relatives gathered for the barbecue that evening; then the younger members of the clan settled into sleeping bags for a night on the lawn, which Silver spent with a cat's purr in her ear and its paws in her face. In the morning, workers arrived to erect a big, striped awning that immediately collapsed and had to be reerected. The tiered cake came to near disaster when Chowder joyously welcomed the bakery lady carrying it. The calf escaped from the pasture and ate two of the decorative bouquets of flowers. The kids got in a battle with the gooey stuff from the bottom of the pond, and a stray mud ball inadvertently clobbered Aunt Emma on a plump cheek.

All in all, Silver thought happily, a typical Sinclair type of celebration. Who needed one Chris Bentley?

Nonrelative guests began arriving about one o'clock; reenactment of the wedding vows followed, then a buffet-style dinner catered by a women's club in town. After that, general collapse. Silver sprawled on the lawn and napped like everyone else.

Toward evening, with sunset turning the ordinary pond to a sheet of red-gold, people started reviving. Silver was trying to decide if she wanted to join a volleyball game that was just starting when she saw someone on the porch whom she hadn't said hi to yet.

She sneaked up behind him and put her hands over his eyes. "Guess who!"

"The girl who once challenged me to arm wrestle to see who'd pay for our milk shakes, and wound up owing me three hamburgers and fries because she just couldn't admit I could beat her until I'd done it four times?"

"Who'd have thought a guy would develop all those muscles just playing chess?" Silver grumbled. Which was what cousin Dale was doing at the moment, his opponent a teenage boy cousin in baggy shorts and backward-turned baseball cap, who, in spite of looking as if he wouldn't know a chessboard from a blackboard, suddenly yelled, "Checkmate!" and shot his fist in the air with a victorious, "Yes!"

"I taught him everything he knows," Dale claimed cheerfully. The boy left to join the volleyball game, and Dale motioned Silver to the empty seat. "Want to play a game?"

"Are you kidding? You know I'd just as soon sit around and watch concrete harden. But hey—I haven't seen you all spring. What have you been doing?"

"Oh, the usual. Although, at the moment, what I'm doing is getting ready to move."

"Oh? New apartment, or buying a house now?" Dale, a certified public accountant, was very well organized financially.

"No, I'm leaving Seattle. I've just accepted a position as head of the accounting department with a big company down in Portland."

Clicks, like the tumblers of a locked safe suddenly falling into place when the right combination of numbers whirl by, suddenly sounded in Silver's head. She took a long look at cousin Dale, mentally stepping back to appraise him with non-cousinly eyes. Nice looking. Intelligent. Quietly witty. Loved the Lord. Financially secure. A man who liked reading about history and browsing antique stores and playing chess. And he was moving to Portland. *Yes!*

"Dale, are you seeing anyone special now?"

"No, not really."

Silver scooted her chair around closer to his and draped an arm around his shoulders. "Dale, have I got a girl for you," she said with feeling. And went on to tell him who and why.

She headed for the volleyball game, feeling suddenly energized. Yes, cousin Dale and the other Silver were right for each other; she could just feel it!

Then she saw a car coming up the long driveway.

Odd. A few stragglers were still leaving, but no one should be just arriving at this late hour. The car hesitated, then eased into the lineup of vehicles remaining on the dust-and-grass area set aside for parking. A tall, dark-haired figure got out.

Chris.

Silver just looked at him, uncertain if she was angry or astonished or glad to see him, uncertain whether she wanted to throw mud balls or run to welcome him. Maybe some of each. Finally she put her feet in motion and walked toward him. A fine dust from the cloud the car had raised on the road drifted around her.

She saw him observing the awning, one corner drooping at half-mast now, the decorative paper on the long tables flapping in the evening breeze. "Looks like I'm a little late." Except for

171

the lack of a tie, he was in office-type clothes, dark slacks and white shirt, but he looked tired and rumpled.

"Well, first things first." If he thought she was going to murmur a soothing *That's okay, glad you could make it,* he could think again. Maybe she was being one-sided and unfair for resenting his putting the business deal first. As he'd pointed out, he couldn't just dump it and blithely chase off cross-country with her. But perhaps this was the time to take a hard look at the facts and consider what life would be like with a driven man who would always have some good, inarguable reason for putting business matters before anything else.

"Big deal with the Golden Lighthouse people all wrapped up?"

"Oh, yes, quite wrapped up."

She drew in a deep breath, biting her tongue to keep from telling Chris how generous he was to grant them all a few minutes of his valuable time after this splendid conquest.

Chris smiled faintly, as if reading her mind…and ruefully acknowledging her right to greet him with a chill that hung in the air like panes of glass ready to fall and shatter. "Perhaps I shouldn't have come after all."

She looked at the unfamiliar car. "Did you drive all the way?

"No. I flew to Spokane and rented the car." He glanced at his watch. "I can probably get back to Spokane in time to catch another plane back yet tonight."

Silver hesitated, not exactly relenting, but feeling a smidgen of guilt for her unwelcoming attitude. From the looks of his clothes, he'd gone straight from final negotiations to the plane, which indicated a certain effort on his part. "Why don't you come in and have something to eat first."

The offer was more grudging than inviting, but he ignored the tone. "Thanks. I'd appreciate that. I haven't had anything since breakfast."

"Did you have any trouble finding us?"

"No. Everybody seems to know where the town's only dentist lives."

She took him through the house to the kitchen, where other people were browsing the leftovers. His presence drew immediate attention, of course, but Silver didn't bother with the niceties of formal introductions. She simply aimed a finger toward various people, attached names, and then, with a casual wave toward Chris, said, "I'd like all of you to meet Chris Bentley, a friend of mine from Seattle." She was tempted to add *Mighty Motel Mogul* but restrained herself.

She was just getting a plate from the stack of Styrofoam supplies when several more people wandered into the kitchen. She heard the bubbling voice of Great-aunt Esther, who always said exactly what she thought, exclaim to him, "Why, you must be Silver's young man! My, you're quite a hunk, aren't you?"

Silver didn't know which embarrassed her more, Esther referring to him as a "hunk" or as "Silver's young man." Chris, however, appeared to take it all in stride and said something Silver didn't catch that made Esther giggle like a girl.

Silver didn't feel like eating again already, but she watched Chris heap a plate with food, poured a glass of lemonade for herself, and led him to a picnic table in the backyard. He ate without talking, and Silver was also silent. She wasn't inclined to play breathless feminine admirer and beg him for all the details of his amazing conquest, and he didn't seem inclined to gloat about the accomplishment.

He finished off with a big piece of anniversary cake, pushed the plate away, and looked at his watch again. "I guess I'd better start back."

"Did you bring a sleeping bag?"

"Yes."

"You may as well throw it down somewhere in the guys'

173

area, then." Just to make certain he realized she wasn't inviting him to stay because she wanted his company, she added, "No point in driving when it's late and you're tired."

"Thank you for your concern."

She glanced at him sharply, but if he was being sarcastic, he hid it behind a final gulp of lemonade.

Just then her motorcycle-enthusiast brother, apparently looking for them, strode across the backyard. "Hey, I hear you have a Gold Wing," he said.

Silver groaned. What did her family do, send out résumés? But the men's conversation about motorcycles kept her and Chris from having to talk, and then her parents came out to meet him. By the time Silver and Chris were alone again, the stars were out, crickets chirping enthusiastically, and he said he thought he'd turn in for the night. Silver showed him where to put his sleeping bag.

Morning was a general madhouse as everyone got ready for Sunday school and church. At church, in the general confusion of finding seats, Silver wound up sitting two pews away from Chris, which suited her fine. Afterward, she reluctantly decided it was time to start home and sought out Chris to tell him she was leaving.

"If you don't mind, I could drop the rental car off in Spokane and ride the rest of the way home with you."

She hesitated, both surprised and uneasy about the request. Did she want to spend all those hours alone with him in the car? "Flying would get you home a lot sooner. So you'd be all rested and bright-eyed, ready to take over your new empire in the morning."

He shrugged. "I'm in no hurry."

Sixteen

Chris tossed his sleeping bag and overnight case into the backseat of Silver's car and slid into the passenger seat beside her. Maybe this wasn't such a good idea after all. Perhaps he should simply have flown back to Seattle after turning in the rental car here at the Spokane airport. But he'd wanted to be with her. He was still almost dazed by what had happened. Dazed and discouraged and angry, mostly with himself.

Although, from the remote look on Silver's lightly sunburned face, she wasn't all that eager to be with him. After a half hour of driving through the wheat fields of eastern Washington, during which she treated him to a single stony line saying there were drinks in the cooler on the backseat, he decided he'd just lie back and close his eyes for a while. He reached for the lever on his seat, but just then she finally muttered something.

"I appreciate your last-minute effort to come to the reunion. It entailed a certain sacrifice on your part, I suppose." Her words and tone wavered between conciliatory and grudging.

He took his hand off the seat lever. "You've jumped to a mistaken conclusion."

Her gaze briefly flicked from the highway to him. "What do you mean?"

"The deal collapsed."

Another shift of gaze, this one shocked. "What?"

"*Finis.* Over. Dead as the proverbial doornail."

She looked disbelieving. "What happened?"

"The heirs of the Golden Lighthouse chain have been squabbling among themselves ever since the death of the old man who founded the chain. As I told you earlier, I'd already bought the share of an heir from back east who was eager to get out. I'd thought this would give me a good inside track from which to buy out the other heirs. But most of them didn't know about this until we got down to final negotiations, and when they did find out, everything exploded.

"It seems that heir was the most disliked in the family, and everyone was furious with her for jumping the gun on the sale. Then they turned furious with me for what they perceived as sneaking around behind their backs. In a sudden show of noble family unity they stopped squabbling and banded together against me, the predatory outsider. They decided to keep the motel chain and let a grandson run it."

"Oh, Chris, after you've worked so long and hard on this!"

"And I've only myself to blame! That's the hard part to swallow. If I hadn't made the misjudgment of rushing in and buying that one heir's share, everything would have been fine. It was a stupid, overeager move." He pounded his fist on his thigh in frustration.

"Chris, don't be so hard on yourself—"

"But Ben won't be surprised, of course."

"Ben?" She repeated the name, taking a moment to place it. "Oh, your grandfather." She glanced at him, apparently puzzled about what Chris's grandfather had to do with this but uncertain about prying. A little tentatively she asked, "How is he now?"

"Quite lucid the last time I visited him. Asking how the deal was progressing. That was another mistake, of course, telling him about it before everything was final."

"I'm sure he'll be sympathetic when he learns what happened."

"No, sympathetic is not what he'll be." Of that Chris was quite certain.

Again her eyes flicked from wide, dark ribbon of highway to him. "You're saying he wanted you to fail?" That possibility sounded startling, even incomprehensible, to her. Which it was, given her warm, loving family.

Chris rested his arm on the open window, letting the rush of air cool his damp palm while he considered what Silver had asked. She slowed the car as they entered a small town, where a cluster of tall metal cylinders for storing wheat gleamed in the sun, then speeded up again.

"No, not necessarily wanted," he finally conceded, although he wouldn't put wanting him to fail past old Ben. "Expected, I suppose."

"I don't understand."

And she wouldn't, of course. He'd met her family only briefly, but he could see how close-knit they were, teasing and even competitive but never mean-spirited or unsupportive. He studied Silver's profile: sandy blond hair that never looked as if she quite had it under control, now even more tousled by the wind whipping through the open window, pert nose, fair skin with a few appealing freckles, mouth that was firm and determined yet so easily broke into laughter. She was far from laughter now, however.

A little hesitantly she added, "Could it be that with all this the Lord is saying something to you about how you're so driven to succeed?"

"Driven?" The unexpected word brought him up short.

"Yes. Driven. I've never understood it. You don't seem all that captivated by material things or a luxurious lifestyle, not particularly concerned with impressing people with how successful you are. Yet everything seems to take second place to achievement of that success."

"I'm not doing it to impress people. I just—" He broke off. No, that wasn't true. There was one person he wanted to impress. One person he'd been trying for years to impress. And never succeeded.

Almost without realizing it, his fingertips brushed that thin white scar angled across his temple, still faintly numb after all these years. Yet it was the inner scars, unseen scars, that had always been more difficult to deal with than this surface brand.

Again he studied Silver. He was falling in love with her, he knew, falling in love with her spirit and idealism, her good humor and occasional fiery temper, her generosity and sweetness. Falling in love because they shared a faith in their Lord and Savior. Falling in love because of their passion for the outdoors and because they had fun doing things together...just being together. And because he could see himself spending the rest of his life with her.

For the first time since he'd left boyhood behind and become a man, he realized that he really wanted to share with someone...share with her...this part of his past that he usually kept walled off even in his own mind.

"Would you like to hear the story of my life?"

The out-of-the-blue question obviously startled her, but her answer was quick and definite. "Yes."

Again he absentmindedly stroked the scar as he considered where to begin. Apparently he was silent longer than he realized, and Silver gave him a little verbal nudge.

"I know that you were born in the Midwest and that your father was a pastor."

"I don't really remember much about being a little kid," he reflected.

"I remember thinking the time would never come when I'd be big enough to go to school." Silver's words were about herself, but he recognized them as a subtle encouragement to delve into his own memories.

He gazed out the open window, the rolling hills of wheat reminding him of similar scenes from his Midwestern childhood. The fields of grain stretching to the horizon were flatter there, but the immense blue sky was the same.

"It seems as if it was always summer when I was little," he said slowly. "I remember being barefoot, squirming my feet so the dust came up between my toes. Feeding the chickens with my mother. Fishing for catfish with my dad in a pond near the house, and my mother bringing us fried chicken for a picnic."

His words quickened as things he hadn't thought about in years came back to him. "I remember thunderstorms on the plains and the lightning scaring and fascinating me at the same time. I remember looking up with awe at my father, who always seemed so much bigger on Sundays when he was preaching from the pulpit." He smiled ruefully. "Although sometimes I was thinking more about the piece of butterscotch candy in my pocket than about the message."

Those small-boy memories had an odd, distinct separateness about them, however, as if they were old photos in an album rather than real memories. But a haze of contentment, like a veil of golden dust, hung over them. Sorrow was yet unknown, death a faraway stranger noticed only when his father conducted a funeral for some old person. And then a wonderful memory: his mother's body growing large and round, and sometimes she'd put his hand on her abdomen so he could feel the astonishing movements of the baby growing inside.

"My brother Brian was born just after my fifth birthday, and I thought he was a special birthday present just for me." He'd been so happy about the new baby, so fascinated by baby toes and fingers and the toothless grin. He paused and swallowed. "But a month later my mother was dead. Killed by a drunk driver as she crossed the road right in front of our house."

"Oh, Chris…" Silver shook her head, her quick, shocked sympathy bringing a tear that trickled down her cheek. She brushed it away, then reached across the seat and squeezed his hand. "I'm so sorry. I had no idea."

"We stayed there another year or so, and then my father had the chance to pastor a church in southwestern Washington. I knew he was glad to get far away from seeing that spot every day where my mother had died. I was, too. It was in this new town that he met my stepmother, who was in her first year of teaching school."

Silver shot him a quick glance. "Did you object to her? Not want her taking your mother's place?"

"Oh, no. I never really thought of her as a stepmother. Her name was Laura, and she was simply another mother, a wonderful woman. But her parents, Ben and Mara, were strongly opposed to her marrying my father. They didn't want her taking on a couple of boys to raise, and they especially didn't want her marrying a preacher, who would never be able, in their estimation, to provide properly for her."

"Apparently she wasn't concerned about that."

"No. And I didn't know anything about this at the time. I thought everything was wonderful. It wasn't until later, when my folks decided to enter the mission field, that I found out about it. Ben came to the house and ranted and raved, saying that my father had no right to drag his daughter off to some primitive jungle, that she deserved better than that, and on and on. To hear him yell it, his daughter had married the world's most irresponsible, worthless man alive." He swallowed, still remembering his small-boy panic at the furious thunder of Ben's voice as he crouched hidden on the steps, listening. "I thought it meant my new mother would leave."

"But she didn't."

"No. I think my dad would just have gritted his teeth and taken whatever Ben handed out, but Mom told Ben if he was going to talk like that then he was no longer welcome in our home, and he stormed out." He paused. "I don't think she and her parents ever saw each other again."

Silver's glance was curious. "And then—?"

"My parents were in training for a while and then we went to Guatemala, where they were assistants at a mission for a year. After that we reopened a mission in a remote area of Brazil that had been closed for a year because of some problems."

"Problems?" He heard an apprehension in her voice, as if she suddenly suspected something bad was coming. Which it was. An old, familiar tension, like spiders crawling across his belly, made him shift uncomfortably in the seat.

But living at the primitive mission had been wonderful for a while. He smiled, remembering the good part. "I was ten or eleven by then, and living in the jungle was every boy's dream of adventure. Brian and I even had a pet baby monkey. The church had been burned, but my father and some of the faithful natives rebuilt it, and I helped too, when I wasn't off playing jungle explorer."

"Swinging through the trees like a miniature Tarzan?" She smiled lightly, as if she could picture him doing that.

"Whenever I could. But I had other things to do, too. My folks had training in the local language before we went there, but I actually learned to use it faster because of contact with the kids. So I could talk to them about Jesus myself and sometimes even translate for my parents." He shook his head. "But it's all gone. I couldn't tell you a single word of the language now."

"Time erases things we learn but don't continue to use, I think."

Perhaps time was what had done it. Or perhaps he'd simply erased it while trying to wipe out everything else about that time.

"What happened there, Chris?" Silver asked softly. He heard the concern and caring in her voice.

"I'm not sure about the background of it. Political unrest, perhaps, along with economic problems and the encroachment of mining and logging interests. Hostility and violence broke out all around us. Looking back, I think the drug trade may also have been involved. There were terrorist threats on the mission, and before long Brian and I could no longer go out and play. I was thirteen then, Brian eight. Sometimes we'd hear gunfire at night, and then there would be reports about people being killed and sometimes even bodies brought into the mission."

"Oh, Chris, how frightening. But your family didn't leave?"

"No. I think my parents considered it. They were concerned about safety for Brian and me. But leaving would have meant abandoning the faithful Christians, who turned out to be the people most persecuted and hated, so it was a real dilemma for them."

"Was your family…persecuted and hated too?"

"We were sitting there about to eat dinner one evening. My father had just finished the prayer when the door flew open. Four men in camouflage clothes, carrying machine guns and machetes, burst in." He swallowed and closed his eyes. The memory was like watching a movie and knowing the terrible scene that was coming next, hoping that this time it wouldn't happen and knowing there was no way to stop it. "One of them shot my father." Shot him enough times with the rapid spitfire of the machine gun to kill an elephant. "Another one sliced my mother's throat with a machete."

He saw her hands go slack on the steering wheel, as if stunned shock at his blunt words had turned them numb. Automatically his own hand reached out to steady the wheel. She turned her face to his and swallowed convulsively, curiosity swallowed up in shock and horror now. "Oh, Chris, no—"

He went on with the grim facts. "The one with the machete turned and hit me next." He was incapable of not touching the scar when he said that, and the thin line felt strangely hard and cold against his fingertips, as if it had a bitter memory of its own. "It must not have been a full blow, or it would have killed me. Maybe they thought I was dead because I fell under the table." Or maybe they didn't care because they had other murderous plans.

She'd gotten a grip on both herself and the steering wheel now. Maybe too tight a grip. Her knuckles stood out white. "Your brother?"

"I don't know who hit him or what happened, but he was already lying on the floor and bleeding from the corner of his mouth. I dragged him under the table with me and covered him with my body, and we just stayed there while the men tore the house apart." And his mother's blood silently dripped off the table into a red pool beside them. He shuddered and jerked himself away from the horror of that memory, unwilling to share it even with Silver.

"Then the men ran out of the house, and a minute later I heard something crackling and smelled smoke. They'd set the house on fire. I dragged Brian toward the back door."

"You couldn't have been more than half-conscious yourself!"

Yes. But conscious enough to make a decision.

"As soon as I opened the door, a bullet smashed through it." The jungle house had been flimsy, and he remembered the flames behind him searing his back, burning like a gasoline-soaked torch. They could have stayed where they were and gone up in flames with the house. Or they could have staggered outside to be shot. Did he pray? Probably. Then he had made the grim decision and had pushed the door open again.

"It was perhaps a hundred and fifty feet from the house to the edge of the jungle. I just put my head down and kept dragging Brian while the bullets tore up the ground all around us." Why hadn't that rain of metal ripped them to shreds? Perhaps because the men were simply playing with them, not really caring if they escaped because two missionary boys could never survive in the jungle. Or maybe the Lord was protecting them, raising a barrier that not even machine-gun bullets could penetrate.

"Finally the men left, but we stayed hidden, watching the house and church and other buildings burn." And watching the jungle, which had once been a wonderful place to play, turn dark and menacing.

"Your family were the only ones at the mission?"

"No. There was an older couple, and a single man named Mike, plus several natives who lived and worked there. When we finally ventured out the next morning, we found their bodies. They'd all been hacked to death. Probably before the men attacked us, I think."

Another swallow moved convulsively up her slim throat. He shouldn't have hit her with this all at once, he thought. It was too brutal, too savage. But there was really no other way to tell it. "What did you do?"

"By then we realized Brian had slashed his foot on something in the jungle. He couldn't walk, so I found a board and rope that had escaped the fire, and I rigged them so I could pull him. After struggling all day, we reached the closest village, but it was abandoned, except for more bodies. But while we were there, a Christian convert we knew sneaked out of the jungle and took us to where his family was hiding. We lived with them for the next three months, moving every day or two because people told the family that the men with machine guns had heard we were still alive and were looking for us. I've always hoped and prayed, after rescuers came and led us out to safety, that the family didn't suffer for what they'd done to help us."

Silver spread her fingers and rubbed her hands on the steering wheel. She was conscious of what she was doing, guiding the car, glancing occasionally in the rearview mirror, braking for a jackrabbit that scooted across the highway, but her movements were on automatic pilot, her mind still riveted to the horrors Chris had lived through.

"This is what you meant when you once said you had problems with forgiveness when you were a boy."

"Yes."

Silver was suddenly ashamed of her own girlhood resistance to forgiveness, the minor wrongs committed against her that now seemed so frivolous compared to those done to Chris. "But you did forgive those who had done this?"

"I hated them," he said flatly. "For a long time I plotted how I'd go back and find and kill them. But eventually my hatred began to come between me and the Lord, and after a long struggle, I finally let it go. Although I suppose the knowledge that they would eventually have to answer to God for what they had done did play a part in my forgiveness."

"Were you angry with God?"

He tilted his head reflectively. "At the time it was happening, I was too scared to be angry. The Lord was all we had to lean on during those months we were running and hiding. Later I was angry, but eventually I was able to let that go, too."

Silver shook her head. She'd read of events such as this, terrible atrocities done to missionaries in far-off places. Yet actually hearing the firsthand account of someone who had lived through it was different. She glanced sideways at Chris, where the white line of the scar she'd always been curious about now stood out as a savage link with his past. She frowned lightly, her thoughts unexpectedly darting around a corner.

"Chris, I appreciate your telling me this. I think that I perhaps understand you a little better now." She hesitated, uncertain how to put into words what she was thinking without sounding hard-hearted and insensitive. He'd lived through a terrible time, seen his parents murdered, and, no more than a child himself, fiercely protected and cared for his brother.

"I can see why you might have a greater concern for security than many people," she said softly. "But I still don't see the connection between this and the way you're so driven to succeed. It just doesn't seem like a reason to be wrapped up in such fierce ambition to build a motel empire."

She thought the comment might anger him. He usually did not take kindly to her use of the word *empire*. But now he simply nodded agreement.

"True." He reached into the cooler in the backseat for a bottle of the mineral water she had stashed there and turned the cap slowly. "But there's more."

Silver simply waited for him to go on.

"Word didn't get back to the States immediately about what had happened at the mission, but eventually Ben got a fragmented report. He went through all the proper channels with the State Department, trying to get something done, but when nothing happened, he took action on his own. He borrowed on everything he owned—he had the beginnings of a motel chain himself, then—and raised enough money to go to Brazil and hire a high-priced band of mercenaries to find us." He paused. "Although at that time, the information was so sketchy that the possibility existed that his daughter was still alive. He didn't know then that Brian and I were the only survivors."

"Are you saying he might not have done it if he'd known that?" Silver was uncertain if the dismay she felt was directed at grandfather Ben for that possibility or at Chris for suggesting it, and he didn't answer the question.

"The men he'd hired found us. Then he brought us back to the States."

"And raised you, even though, technically, you weren't related to him."

"Yes. He and my step-grandmother could have dumped us on the authorities to live in a foster home. But they didn't do that. They fed and clothed and educated us. We had proper medical care. My wound had healed on its own, but by the time we got back to the States, Brian's foot was badly infected and needed expensive surgery, and they never hesitated about that. They gave us all the things most kids have: bicycles, allowances, sports equipment, a TV of our own. There were household rules and discipline, but they weren't unreasonable or unnecessarily strict."

Silver hesitated, hearing love and gratitude in Chris's listing of all his step-grandparents had done. She was also aware that one more word, loud and clear, lurked in there. "But—?"

"But Ben was a bitter and angry man. He wound up unable to repay all he'd borrowed to mount the rescue, and he lost almost everything."

"Surely he didn't blame you and Brian for that!"

"No." Chris's answer was again emphatic. "But he blamed our father. He blamed our father and religion for everything, especially his daughter's death. In fact, he seemed to blame Dad more than the men who actually committed the murders. And he never let up on Dad or religion. We heard it over and over. If our father had stayed in the States instead of chasing off to preach to a bunch of dirty savages, none of this would have happened. If Dad had taken his nose out of his Bible once in a while, he could have amounted to something. If Dad had had any sense about money, if he hadn't been so wrapped up in a lot of religious nonsense, he wouldn't have left us, his sons, destitute."

"Oh, Chris!"

"Ben never directly attacked or criticized Brian and me, but every time he tore into Dad, which was often, even after Dad was long dead, I also felt responsible for everything that had happened."

"What about your faith? Did he try to turn you away from it?"

"He ridiculed it mostly. He'd never been a religious man, and he hadn't wanted his daughter to marry a preacher, although that was more an economic thing, I think, than an open hostility to religious beliefs. But after his daughter's death, he fervently hated and scorned anything to do with God or church, turning almost fanatic about it.

"Sometimes he'd deliberately come up with fun things to do on Sunday to try to entice us away from church. But he never actually forbid us to go, never banned our Bibles from the house." Chris smiled without humor. "Perhaps, in a way, the things he said and did actually backfired because the more he criticized Dad and religion, the more determined I was to stick to it. And somewhere in there I started vowing that when I grew up I'd prove to him that a man could be a faithful Christian and a financial success, too. I wanted to prove my worth and somehow, through that, also prove my father's worth to him."

The lightbulb of understanding finally clicked on in Silver's mind. *Driven.* Was it any wonder?

"From the time we started living with them, I worked in the one small motel Ben still owned, helping with the cleaning and yard work, and in the summer after I graduated from high school, when Grandma had a stroke and Ben spent most of his time caring for her, I took over running it. A motel across town came up for sale, and I figured a way we could expand by second-mortgaging the first one and using the money to make a down payment on the other motel.

"I thought Ben would be pleased and impressed with my initiative and astute business acumen. But when I told him about my great idea, he just laughed at me, told me I had no better financial sense than my father, that I couldn't turn a dime into a dollar if someone gave me a minting machine."

"Oh, Chris," Silver repeated, feeling so helpless, so hurt for him. Yet curious, too. "So...how did you get started?"

"When Grandma died a few weeks later, Ben was more bitter and unhappy than ever. He couldn't blame her death on my father, but he could blame it on my father's God. Even if he didn't really believe that God existed. Anyway, he told me I could just have the motel, do with it as I pleased, that it didn't matter to him anymore. He had his Social Security check, and that was all he needed. Then he sat back to watch me fail."

"But you didn't fail."

"No. I managed to get the second motel, and after that I just kept going. But in Ben's eyes I never succeeded, either. I never managed to convince him that my successes were anything but dumb luck or someone else's mistake, that sooner or later it was all going to collapse. I thought that if I could pull off this big Golden Lighthouse deal, maybe I'd finally prove something to him. But I blew it." He hammered his thigh again. "I just blew it."

His anger with himself was back, and Silver found herself wishing almost fiercely that the deal had succeeded. Her anger was directed at the heirs who had banded against him, a rebellious feeling that she'd like to bang their stubborn heads together.

She moved her shoulders against the seat, feeling suddenly weary and helpless because she couldn't do any more than he could about the collapse of the deal, of course. She was filled with a greater knowledge and understanding now, but she also felt drained emotionally. Chris was perceptive enough to see that.

"Would you like me to drive for a while?" he asked.

"Yes," she said gratefully. "Please."

Seventeen

hris said that it was too far out of Silver's way to take him home, that he could take a cab from her apartment, but she drove him all the way to the condo. He dragged his sleeping bag and overnight case out of the backseat, locked both doors carefully behind him, then came around to her side of the car. She rolled down the window. He leaned through it and kissed her lightly.

"I'll call you in a day or two. We'll do something fun." His smile didn't erase the dark sculpting of shadows on his face. Wryly he added, "Looking on the bright side, I should have a lot more free time now."

Once she probably would have retorted, only half teasing, *Until the next big deal comes along.* But she saw things differently now.

"Tomorrow night," she said swiftly. "My place. Dinner." She swallowed. "Chris, I'm glad you came. I'm glad you talked to me."

His eyes met hers in the shadows of the car, and she felt the powerful strength of a bond between them that had not been there before. "So am I. But there's something I have to do tomorrow night."

"Oh." Had she made a mistake and read something between them that wasn't really there?

He squeezed her shoulder reassuringly. "I have to tell Ben the deal fell through, and I may as well get it over with."

"Chris, if you'd like, I'll come with you—" She broke off, afraid she'd jumped in where she shouldn't have, but after a momentary pause of surprise, he nodded.

She thought he was simply going to squeeze her shoulder again, but he leaned through the window and kissed her, harder this time, his hand wrapping around the back of her neck almost fiercely, his mouth moving against hers with a passion and intensity that made her clutch the seat with both hands. She had a strange feeling of being caught in a powerful undercurrent.

Abruptly he lifted his head, his gaze meeting hers. Then his head dipped briefly to hers again, the light touch of his lips putting a punctuation mark on the incendiary feelings suddenly ignited between them. She swallowed, grateful for his good sense and control, and pressed her cheek against his hand. He stepped back and lightly rapped the window frame with his knuckles.

"I'll pick you up about six-thirty tomorrow night. We'll get something to eat afterwards."

That Chris, whose appetite seldom faltered, didn't want to eat first said something about his nerves in connection with this meeting.

Silver drove home with a strange mixture of emotions crashing around inside her. A feeling for Chris that was now so close to being in love that claiming she wasn't in love was toying with the truth. Hurting because he had known such hurt as a child.

Burning with a hot resentment toward Ben, a fierce desire that Chris could somehow prove both his and his father's worth to the stubborn old man. She even cast around for ways to do that. Take Ben out to see the construction on the impressive new motel at Bothell? Give him a grand tour of every motel in the Maraben Inns chain? Look for a different chain to buy to replace the collapsed Golden Lighthouse deal?

The following evening, she was still thinking such thoughts when the phone rang as she was slipping into a summery cotton dress for the visit to Ben. It was a woman at church who said she had driven out to see the billboard, was equally indignant about it, and wanted the address Silver had located to write the company in protest. The call lifted Silver's spirits. That project was on track anyway.

She finished dressing, adding white summer sandals and whimsical daisy earrings. Her own misgivings about this meeting were growing, but she wasn't about to back out. She wanted Ben to know that no matter what he thought, there were others who admired Chris, people who respected all he'd accomplished, who thought he was a financial genius.

Chris arrived, kissed her once on the cheek, smiled, and did a more thorough job with another kiss. Then he held her hands in his, stepped back, and looked her up and down with complete approval.

"Ben will like the dress. He never has quite accepted the idea of women in pants. Grandma always wore a dress."

"Frankly," Silver said with a flash of spirit, "I don't really care if he likes me *or* my dress."

The home where Ben now lived was south of Seattle, in the Renton area. The middle-aged woman who operated the family-style residence, for which Silver knew Chris undoubtedly paid a hefty monthly sum, smiled ruefully when she let them in.

"I'm afraid Ben's mood is a bit grumpy. He's been holed up in his room all day. But perhaps your visit will cheer him up."

"Not likely," Chris muttered under his breath as he led Silver down the hallway to Ben's room. He rapped on the closed door. The response was something between a grumble and a growl. "That's probably as close to a welcome as we're going to get." He pushed the door open.

Silver peered inside. Ben was sitting in a comfortable easy chair, scowling at a sitcom on TV. Nothing out of the ordinary about that, she granted him. Sometimes she scowled at the silly things, too. He was smaller and slighter in build than she had anticipated, and she realized that she had mentally built him into some kind of oversized ogre. His tan pants and yellow sports shirt were neat, his silver hair combed. The room was large and cheerful, a bright quilt covering the bed, four folding chairs flanking a card table, green plants on the windowsill, and a colorful Navajo blanket on the wall.

"Hi, Ben."

Ben acknowledged Chris's greeting with a nod that, although not the kind of welcome Silver had received from her grandfathers when they were alive, was more indifferent than hostile. He rose from his chair when he saw Silver. A lingering holdover of his innate gentlemanly instincts more than any specific welcome for her, she suspected. His movements were stiff and jerky, with a catch in his knee that made him grab the chair for balance.

Chris made introductions. The name *Silver Sinclair* did not appear to mean anything to Ben, although whether that indicated that Chris had never brought the other Silver here or that Ben didn't remember her, she was uncertain.

"Big deal fall through yet?" he inquired of Chris. There was obviously nothing wrong with his memory on that point. The malicious phrasing, without even the preliminaries of friendly small talk, startled Silver but apparently not Chris.

"Yep, Ben, it sure did. It fell through." Unsaid was the echo, *Just as you expected it would.*

The old man returned to his chair. A wave of his hand vaguely suggested that if they wanted to sit, they could. Chris didn't, and Silver wouldn't have even if he had. She felt like a cat with its back arched, ready to spit and claw.

"What happened?" Ben asked.

Chris told him the details of the collapse, not sparing his own error that had angered the heirs into turning on him en masse. Ben listened without comment. Perhaps, as Chris had granted him, Ben hadn't wanted him to fail. But he certainly had an I-told-you-so air that said all this validated his long held, like-father-like-son scorn. An air not dispelled when he finally said something.

"Would have been quite an accomplishment if you'd pulled it off, I suppose. But these things take real expertise and skill. Not exactly the stuff religion teaches." He suddenly looked at Silver and added with acid bluntness, "It was all that religious folderol that got my daughter killed, you know, Chris's dad dragging her off to the jungle with him to save the savages."

Then he cocked his head at Chris, as if to make certain the jabs had hit home before continuing. "Of course, even if the deal had gone through, you might of just wound up getting took. I remember that shyster insurance outfit your father got tangled up with."

Silver noted how Chris's hands clenched into fists. "No, Ben, this wasn't a shyster deal. It would have been an excellent investment."

"Then maybe the other side was just praying harder than you were. Isn't it the side that prays the loudest and longest and says the most hallelujahs that wins?"

The words were so casually spoken that it took Silver a moment to grasp their taunting, all-inclusive ridicule of Chris, faith, and prayer. She gasped, tempted to stalk out, but Chris sent her a warning glance, and the visit straggled on for another fifteen minutes while Chris gallantly tried to come up with information and observations about the outside world that might interest Ben. Silver ached to storm over and make the old man acknowledge and appreciate how hard Chris was trying. All that kept her from doing it was reminding herself he was not well mentally…plus grabbing the back of a chair and holding on as if it were a flagpole in a high wind.

"Do you need anything?" Chris asked finally, his tone still soft and controlled. "Maybe some of those chocolate bars you used to like?"

"No, don't bother. Nothing tastes like it used to."

The old man stood again as Chris took Silver's elbow and nudged her toward the door. She was astonished to hear Ben say, just as if this had been a pleasant, normal social visit instead of a painful humiliation for Chris, "Glad you came. You, too, Miss—" He broke off, and for the first time she saw him struggle with the flaws in his memory functions. She felt an unexpected and unwanted sympathy, a quick desire to tell him that it didn't mean anything—she forgot names, too!—but he simply muttered something under his breath and sat down with his back to them.

She breathed deeply when they were outside on the pleasantly landscaped grounds, surrounded by the scent of freshly mowed lawn. She seethed with anger and resentment at old Ben's attitude.

"What was all that stuff about the shyster insurance company?"

"Dad had a small insurance policy. After his death, the company wound up not having to pay because of some technicality."

"Oh, Chris! He's rubbing that into *you* after all these years?"

"His memory never falters on some points."

"May I nominate you for sainthood?" At Chris's astonished blink she managed a strained laugh. "You said once that you didn't visit Ben as often as you should, but you deserve at least sainthood for visiting him at all."

"Thanks, but somehow I doubt you're eligible for sainthood if you're grinding your teeth and clenching your fists every minute of a visit."

"Perhaps not," she admitted. "But I can see now why you've wanted to prove something to him. He's...*infuriating!* He's determined to believe that you're a failure and that faith in God is foolishness. It makes me want to scream at him." Yet she also felt an unwanted pity for Ben lurking under the anger and frustration. He was not unaware of his memory lapses and undoubtedly saw both them and the decrease in his physical capabilities as ominous warning signs. Yet instead of enjoying as much of life as he now could with Chris, instead of finding peace and comfort in Christ, he stubbornly remained inside the bars of his prison of bitterness.

Chris opened the door of the Mercedes for her. He seldom used the big car except for business purposes, and she hadn't even known he owned it for quite a while. Big, expensive cars had never mattered to Silver, but now she rubbed her hands against the leather seat, taking an almost fierce pleasure in the luxurious softness and rich scent. How many people could afford a luxury car such as this? Shouldn't Chris's ownership of one prove something about success to stubborn old Ben?

She really didn't feel like eating much, and apparently Chris felt the same way because he nodded quick agreement when she suggested sandwiches at her apartment.

In the kitchen, they formed a two-person assembly line. Silver spread mayonnaise, ham, and Swiss cheese on the whole wheat bread. Chris added pickles, sliced tomatoes, lettuce, and a dash of a zippy vinaigrette. They sat at her tiny table with coffee.

"What are you going to do now?" Silver asked finally.

"You mean beyond going home and banging my head on the wall in frustration?"

"That's very nonproductive. I know because I've tried it."

He smiled, then shrugged. "I don't know. Just muddle along for a while, I suppose."

"Chris, I doubt you've ever just 'muddled along' in your life."

He refilled their coffee cups. "At this point I don't seem to have much choice."

She pushed her paper plate back and twisted the pottery cup slowly in circular patterns on the table. "Yes, I think you do. A choice is exactly what you have."

His quick lift of head held interest, as if he thought she perhaps had a selection of fresh ideas about how to attack the Golden Lighthouse deal or old Ben's stubbornly negative attitude.

"I almost hate to say this because one part of me just aches to prove something to Ben, and I know if I feel that way, you must feel it a hundred times stronger. But I really think you have to consider that the Lord may be trying to tell you something with the collapse of the Golden Lighthouse deal; that maybe he'd like to see you give less of your life to this assault on ever-greater success and more to him."

"I can do more for the Lord's causes by earning and giving generously than I ever could by putting in an extra hour or two on some church project myself!"

"But that's your viewpoint, not the Lord's, and maybe it isn't what he wants. Sometimes we mistake our desires or will for the Lord's will, and then he has to throw up roadblocks to make us change our paths. I think of that verse in Hebrews that says no discipline seems pleasant at the time, but that later it produces a harvest of peace and righteousness."

"This isn't just a roadblock," Chris muttered. "This is like a thousand-foot wall just popped up in front of me."

"It takes bigger roadblocks to snag some people's attention. To get yours, it's a wonder the Lord didn't hopscotch Mount Everest across an ocean or two and drop it in your pathway. You may not be related by blood to Ben, but you certainly have some of the same stubbornness."

Chris scowled at the blunt, not overly sympathetic words. "What are you suggesting, that God wants me to drop everything and become a missionary like my folks?"

"No. But you might consider dropping everything long enough to be a tent counselor at our summer camp. You might volunteer for committee work at your church. You might give time to some church projects. You might throw your weight behind getting rid of that sleazy billboard."

"I might."

The growled response held all the enthusiasm of a man who has anticipated owning a new Ferrari but instead finds himself with a rusted-out Vega missing one fender.

Eighteen

hris called two days later. "Exactly what does a tent counselor do?" he demanded without preliminaries.

"Stay with the boys in a tent at night, of course. Make sure they clean up and brush their teeth. See that they don't inflict bodily harm on themselves or each other—"

"In other words, a glorified baby-sitter."

"There's more to it than that! Counselors also teach or assist with classes, lead recreation activities, and sit with the kids at mealtimes to keep them in line. But maybe the most important part is reflecting Christ in your life in a way that makes faith a part of daily living. Things sometimes come across better to kids when they learn them in everyday action. We get kids from Christian homes, but we also get kids whose homes are totally empty spiritually."

Long silence, then a muttered, "Okay, I'll do it," as if he were agreeing to a week of dental surgery.

Silver ignored the lack of enthusiasm. "Chris, that's wonderful! We'll have a great time."

After Silver got him officially signed up and they attended a couple of orientation meetings, plus a tent-inspection-and-mending session, his interest perked up, and he actually showed some real enthusiasm for the project. He surprised Silver by offhandedly mentioning that he had a lifeguard's certificate and offering to act as a lifeguard for the swimming area, an offer eagerly accepted because one of the two men who had been lifeguards last year couldn't come this year. A position on the budget committee at his church opened up, and he volunteered for that. He told Mrs. Oliver about the billboard, and she and several other secretaries wrote protest letters. He never talked about the collapse of the Golden Lighthouse deal, but Silver knew that in spite of the changes he'd made in his life schedule to make more time for the Lord's work…and her…that he still regarded it as a personal failure.

"See, doesn't giving something of your time and yourself to the Lord feel good?" Silver inquired as they walked out of church together one evening. He'd started attending Wednesday night prayer meetings at Silver's church with her. The day had been a scorcher by Seattle standards, and the asphalt parking lot still radiated heat on her bare legs.

"Yeah, I guess it does," he admitted. "But I also have another personal project in mind, something I've been meaning to do for a long time."

"Which is?"

"Doing something with my condo so I don't feel as if I'm living in a display model titled 'Interior Decorator's Nightmare.'"

Silver didn't comment, although she silently agreed that was an apt description of the condo at present. "You must have an interior decorator who does your motels."

"Actually, I thought you and I might do the condo."

Silver stopped short a few feet from the pickup. "I don't know anything about interior decorating! My place, after the expensive stuff I bought back in my credit-card heyday was repossessed, is done with family discards and yard-sale stuff."

"But you picked the *right* yard-sale stuff and family-discard pieces. I can sit there and feel soothed. Comfortable."

"But what's right for my tiny apartment wouldn't be right for your condo."

"See, you do know something about interior decoration! Also, there's another good reason you should help pick the furnishings."

"What's that?"

"You may have to live with them, so you'd better choose something you like." He grinned, adding so quickly that she wasn't certain she'd heard what she thought she'd heard, "Want to stop for an iced latte on the way home?"

Or if she had heard correctly, perhaps he realized it implied something he didn't want to imply and that was why he hurried on to iced latte as an instant diversion. Or perhaps she had heard correctly, and it meant exactly what it sounded as if it meant.

She waited a heartbeat, but he didn't expand the tantalizing comment, and she quickly said, "Sure, an iced latte would be great."

He invited her over the following evening, and together they took a general inventory of what the condo needed. New dining table and chairs, large-scale living-room furniture to get rid of that island-in-an-uncharted-sea look, plus complete furnishings for the guest bedroom, which now held a broken weight-lifting machine, assorted sports equipment, and various overflowing boxes of miscellaneous stuff. He planned to leave the den, which held his computer and filing cabinets, unchanged, but the master bedroom also needed a complete overhaul.

Silver began their first decorating expedition by asking the basic question, "What style of furniture and colors do you like?"

They were standing by a store display of sofas and love seats done in a wild floral-and-fish fabric that looked like some mad scientist's aquarium after an experiment gone bad, and to her relief Chris said emphatically, "I'm not positive about what I do want, but I know it isn't *that.*"

They wandered on, through forests of lamps large and small, then an area of modernistic, hard plastic stuff with chairs shaped like giant cupped hands. The store was so huge that it felt as if they were on some vast open range surrounded by roaming herds of sofas and overstuffed chairs rather than livestock.

"I like clean lines, not fussy or doodady," Chris stated after they finally found their way out of the plastic maze. "Dramatic colors but not flamboyant. Contemporary styling but not cold and hard. Real wood and leather and…soft stuff that feels nice." He sounded a bit embarrassed when he said that, as if it went against his macho-male character, but Silver knew what he meant. "What do *you* like?" he asked.

"What I like isn't important."

"Yes, it is."

Silver gave herself a quick mental thumping. What was she trying to do with that skittish little statement, slyly wangle some declaration of undying love and happily-ever-after out of him right here beside an ottoman shaped like an elephant's foot? "Hey, what about this?" she asked, relieved to be able to sidestep this discussion with a rush to something she actually liked. Thought *he'd* like, she corrected.

"Actually, my 'interior decorator's nightmare' isn't looking so bad at this point," he muttered. Then he spotted what she was inspecting, a walnut pedestal stand for a television set, utilitarian but also sleek and graceful. "Hey, that's more like it!"

After buying the pedestal stand, they didn't find anything

else they liked there, but over the course of two Saturdays and a dozen stores, they put together several roomfuls of furniture. Chris had everything delivered, and on a Tuesday evening he invited her over to view the results.

"Oh, yes!" she breathed as she turned in a circle in the living room. The condo perhaps still didn't qualify as "decorated." It didn't have the finishing touches that a real decorator would give it, but the basics were there.

Elegant but not pretentious, dramatic but not theatrical. The huddled-island look was gone, but the rooms still offered space and light and air, not a fussy clutter of furniture. The two off-white sectionals, separated by a walnut-framed, glass-topped table, took full advantage of the spectacular views. A random scattering of hunter green and burgundy pillows added a dramatic flair. The television floated serenely on its pedestal stand. Walnut bookshelves lined one corner of the room, empty except for an oversized, open Bible with a red satin bookmark, a half shelf of Christian books, and a few volumes on business management. The salesman had suggested that some people bought books "by the foot" to fill shelves decoratively, but with a single exchanged glance, Silver and Chris had silently agreed that books were to be selected individually, with loving care.

"It all looks fantastic, except—" Silver moved one of the suede easy chairs six inches to the left and straightened a misty watercolor of the Seattle waterfront in the early 1900s by a fraction of an inch. Chris had said he'd bought the painting several years ago, but it had just been leaning against the wall of his bedroom until now.

"Just what it needed," Chris declared, his tone teasing her picky adjustments. "I knew there was something not quite right, but I just couldn't figure out what it was."

"Make fun of me, and I won't give you my housewarming present," Silver warned.

"Present?"

He sounded eager, but she made him wait while she continued her inspection of the condo. She felt a little awkward peeking into the privacy of Chris's bedroom, but she wanted to see how the natural-oak sleigh bed, with its gracefully curved headboard and footboard looked. It and the matching pieces all looked great.

Then she stopped and blinked in astonishment.

"Surprised?" Chris asked, apparently reading the startled expression on her face.

His former bed had been a single, and a single-model sleigh bed had been what they looked at in the store. But this was a generous queen size, topped with a puffy burgundy comforter that looked both luxurious and snuggly.

"I just thought, looking to the future, that this would be more appropriate," he said blandly.

She left that statement unexplored and hurried on to the guest bedroom. There she found another surprise. "A crib!"

"I want to be prepared if Brian and Carol bring the baby to visit sometime."

He'd obviously done a little shopping when she wasn't along, and his initiative pleased her. "You are definitely improving in thoughtfulness and sensitivity," she declared.

He grinned. "I'm working on it."

They went back to the big living room, where Silver handed him the heavy sack she'd brought. He tore off the wrapping with all the eagerness of a ten-year-old birthday boy.

"I know it's nothing you'd ever have bought for yourself."

"It's perfect!"

Without hesitation he set the cast-iron figure of the curled, sleeping cat on the fireplace hearth, exactly where Silver had pictured it. She clapped her hands, delighted with how the cat's homey whimsy and sturdy dignity fit the hearth so well. Chris

206

turned to her, put his hands on her shoulders, and kissed her appreciatively.

"Thanks, Sil. We make a good decorating team, don't you think?" He tilted his head. "A good team in other ways, too."

They looked at each other for a long moment. Was he about to propose? Silver's heart ran a hundred-yard dash within her chest. Did she want him to propose? And, in another rush, came a heady, reckless thought: Who said a man had to be the one to propose?

Hastily, before that thought could leap into impulsive action, she pulled a letter out of her purse. "From the auto-parts company with the billboard ad," she said as she handed the letter to him.

He scanned the brief paragraph quickly. "They 'appreciate your comments,' but they feel the billboard is 'in good taste' and 'inoffensive' and have no intention of removing it." He looked up. "Giving up?"

"No way! That was just the first round, the polite approach appealing to their sense of decency. Now we go to writing the company owning the billboard, letters to the editor, local retail associations, and anyone else we can think of. We might even get around to picketing them if we have to."

He tapped the letter with his other hand, as if giving thoughtful consideration to something, but handed it back without further comment.

"And this also came in the mail today. I think it's good news, but maybe you'll think I stuck my nose into something that was none of my business."

"Which would be the very first time you've ever done that, of course," he teased lightly. But a scowl line formed between his heavy eyebrows as he read the handwritten note she'd received from the other Silver. "You've been matchmaking, I take it?"

"They just seemed so right for each other."

"Just who is this guy she's thanking you so enthusiastically for sending her way?"

"He's my cousin, Dale Willetson. He was at the anniversary reunion, although you probably didn't meet him. He's a steady, responsible guy. He's something of an intellectual, plays chess, and likes antiques...." Her voice trailed off as Chris reread the letter and continued to scowl. "Do you mind that I suggested he get in touch with her when he moved to Portland?"

Chris tilted his head thoughtfully, his blue eyes appraising. "What you're really asking is, am I still interested in her?"

Silver hadn't openly let herself think about it in those blunt terms, but, yes, deep down, she did wonder if there was still something that might eventually draw Chris and the other Silver together again.

He put his hands on her shoulders. "Sil, I care about her. I want her to be happy, and I don't want to see her tangled up with some guy who might hurt her. But it's you I'm in love with."

Silver blinked. *It's you I'm in love with.* She'd been waiting, wanting to hear those words. Oh, yes, she had, even though she hadn't let herself admit it! But now that they were here, she simply felt a little dazed, as if a fog had enveloped her head.

"And if you say your cousin Dale is a good guy, then I'm happy for both of them and wish them the very best. Now I think we should discuss something else."

"What?"

"Us."

She repeated the word as if it were some unfamiliar foreign phrase. "Us?"

"I planned to do this more romantically, with flowers and candlelight and a ring I could whip out of my pocket with a dramatic flourish. But..." He paused, smiling tenderly into her eyes. "Will you marry me, Sil?"

Silver couldn't think of a single romantic or memorable thing to say, so she simply breathed what was in her heart. "Yes. Oh, yes!" Then, before she could stop herself, another word blurted out. "When?"

She felt the instant blaze of a blush, but Chris grinned. "That's another thing I love about you. No coy beating around the bush. You cut right to the bottom line." He pulled her over to the new sectional sofa. "So let's sit down and decide *when*."

"I wasn't implying that we should rush out and get married this instant."

He leaned over and kissed the tip of her nose. "Sounds like a terrific idea to me. Buy the rings, get the license and blood tests tomorrow, grab the minister, and take a honeymoon!"

His eagerness was flattering…and tempting! But Silver shook her head. "I don't care about some big, elaborate wedding with a cast of thousands, but my folks would be hurt if we did it without them. And I can't just take off from work that abruptly. Also, your brother and his wife and Ben might like to come."

"Ben!"

"He has his faults, I know, but he raised you."

"I can do without Ben on my wedding day," Chris stated flatly. "But how's this for a plan?"

With his usual efficient, "crash straight from point A to point B" thinking, Chris did indeed have an instant plan. The week-long summer camp was coming up in two weeks; they'd fulfill their commitment to it and return to Seattle on the Saturday camp ended. They'd have the ceremony on Sunday, squeezed in whenever the minister could manage, and leave immediately afterward on a week-long honeymoon.

"Will that be time enough for your parents to arrange to come to Seattle?"

209

Silver was still trying to digest the whirlwind schedule, but she managed to say, "Yes, I think so."

"Any preferences for a honeymoon?"

A wedding. A honeymoon. Oh yes, and summer camp was in there, too.

And at one time she had been wondering what she'd do on her vacation this year!

Chris grinned. "You look as if you're in shock. We'll decide on a honeymoon destination later." He paused. "Or maybe, since we both know my insensitive-clod tendencies, I'm rushing you into something you don't really want to do?"

"I want to do this!" The words tumbled out so quickly that he laughed delightedly.

"I'm glad to hear that. Just one more thing, if I haven't already made it plain enough. I love you, Sil." His voice turned husky, and his hands framed her face as he repeated the words. "Oh, how I love you!"

Silver felt the sting of tears fill her eyes. For a moment she couldn't speak. Finally, she whispered, "I love you, Chris."

He laughed softly. "Did you think, the first time we met, that you'd ever hear yourself saying those words?"

"Did you picture yourself marrying the woman who dumped hot espresso all over you?"

They laughed together, and then they stopped laughing and his arms encircled her for a long kiss of love and tenderness and promise.

Silver had never believed the phrase *walking on air* had any basis in reality, but as she floated home that night and into the office the next morning, she changed her mind. Perhaps gravity was merely a state of mind, she thought with a certain giddiness, not some unbreakable physical law.

At the office, however, she discovered that even in the heady stratosphere of happiness, earthly obstacles loomed. And she collided head-on with one of them.

Nineteen

After the official notification arrived at her desk, Silver had two hours to smolder before she could get in to see Mr. Landeau. The meeting with him proved as futile as Chris's efforts to demonstrate his competence and financial worthiness to his stubborn grandfather. She thought about calling Chris immediately but decided to wait so she wouldn't scorch the phone lines. He had a business dinner scheduled for that evening but was coming by for coffee afterwards.

She spent the time before he arrived at the apartment baking cookies, squishing and punching the dough with her bare hands in a hyperactive effort to work off some of her frustration. A futile effort because she kept wishing it were Mr. Landeau's skimpy hair rather than cookie dough that she was yanking and pulling.

It took Chris all of thirty seconds after his arrival and kiss to discern that all was not right here. "What's wrong?"

It was a sensitivity she appreciated even as she fumed. She gave him coffee and a cookie with the incriminating imprint of a fist mark.

"Mr. Landeau sent an office memo this morning advising that my vacation time has been switched to September."

"But your scheduled time is less than two weeks off! Can he do that?"

"Apparently he's done it." She paced the limited space in her tiny living room. Four steps, whirl. Four steps, whirl, and repeat.

Chris retreated to the safer area of the kitchen. He leaned his elbows on the counter separating kitchen from living room, his hands protecting his coffee cup as if it could be in danger. "He did this just to you, or to other members of the staff also?"

"Just me. He said it was my two weeks that had to be rescheduled because other staff members scheduled for that time had children and couldn't change to September because of school."

"And the fact that you have summer camp *and* a wedding planned was irrelevant?"

"Totally." She paused in her frustrated pacing. "I have nothing but suspicious feelings to go on, of course, but I think he picked me because he liked the idea of throwing a wrench into my camp plans. He's not exactly Booster of the Year for Christian activities." She also suspected Mr. Landeau had been lying in wait for her ever since their unpleasant scene over Karyn Anderson's temporary stay here in the apartment. She'd forced him to back off that time, and now he was taking revenge for her small victory. "Interrupting my wedding plans was just an unexpected bonus."

"Did he justify the change with a reason?"

"He says it's because he has to attend a professional management conference in Alberta, Canada, and the office will be left understaffed unless the vacation schedule is changed. If I'm so invaluable that I have to be there because he isn't, how come *I'm* not making *his* salary?"

Chris lifted a dark eyebrow. "And this conference just

214

sprouted at the last minute? Every professional conference I ever heard of is scheduled months in advance."

"Colleen says some of his buddies are going up there on a golfing junket, and he scrounged around until he found some conference he could use as an excuse so he could go, too."

Chris absentmindedly inspected the odd markings on a cookie. "Postponing our wedding and honeymoon until September isn't exactly convenient." He grinned unexpectedly. "In fact I have the days multiplied out to the exact number of hours until the honeymoon starts. But we *could* do it. Summer camp, however, is not movable."

"Right. And they're already shorthanded this year. I can't drop out at this late date."

"What happens if you just politely tell Mr. Landeau you have commitments that can't be changed, the vacation dates were promised to you, and you're taking them?"

"I presume I wouldn't have a job when I returned."

"If he's really doing this because of some hostility toward your religious beliefs or affiliations, he could be on very shaky legal ground," Chris pointed out thoughtfully. "Is there someone higher up to whom you could protest?"

"There's an invisible board that hires the manager. But I'm sure Mr. Landeau is clever enough that I could never prove he picked on me for some malicious personal reason."

"Then it appears that you have a choice to make." Chris came out from behind the counter and planted himself on the sofa, his elbows on his knees.

Silver stopped in front of him. She nodded thoughtfully. "I can knuckle under, miss camp, and postpone our wedding. Or I can defy him, take my two weeks, and see what happens."

"One point to help in your decision." He snagged her around the waist and pulled her down on his lap. He wrapped his arms around her from behind and rested his chin on her shoulder. "As Mrs. Chris Bentley, you won't exactly be hungry and homeless if you find yourself out of a job. In fact, this may be opportunity, not catastrophe. A little shove from the Lord pushing you to find or create that opportunity with a Christian counseling service that you've wanted."

It was much the same theory that she'd offered him about the collapse of his Golden Lighthouse deal. Crisis could be opportunity, not disaster. "That's a point to consider," she agreed. Although she also had to admit that accepting crisis as opportunity was rather more difficult when it was *she* poised for a long walk on a short gangplank.

He nuzzled her ear lightly as she pondered the situation and weighed her choices.

"Are you trying to influence my decision?" she asked with an attempt at stern disapproval.

He was all innocence as he flung his arms wide. "Who, *me?*"

She turned sideways in his lap and draped her arms around him. "Yes, you."

"Yes, I suppose I am. The 'crash straight from point A to point B' part of me that you are all too familiar with wants to get married *now*. But more important than that, I want you to do what is right between you and the Lord."

She hesitated only a fraction of a heartbeat longer. "Summer camp, the wedding…*and* honeymoon…are on," she promised recklessly, a promise sealed with a kiss. "No postponements. No delays."

The next meeting with Mr. Landeau was short and tense. Silver informed him that because of her previous commitment to the church's summer camp and her wedding, she could not change her plans and was taking her vacation as scheduled. He informed her in formal, superior tones that going ahead with such disregard for management decisions would necessitate termination of her employment.

"Then I may as well give you my resignation, effective at the end of my scheduled vacation time, right now!"

Mr. Landeau's "beady little eyes" narrowed appraisingly, and Silver knew he was trying to decide if he could get away with firing her on the spot and eliminating pay for her vacation time. Apparently he decided to get in a few digs while considering the possibility.

"Ah, yes, I almost forgot. You've snagged this rich and successful fiancé, haven't you? So now you can afford to, as the old saying goes, tell the boss to take this job and shove it."

Silver stifled a gasp at the rather crude phrasing. She dropped her clenched hands to her sides, and with head held stiffly she said, "I arranged for this vacation time weeks ago, and I'm entitled to it. I promised to help with my church's summer camp, and I fully intend to keep that promise." The challenge hung in the air like an arrow stopped in flight. Would he dare fire her right now?

But would she—Silver had to ask herself uneasily as Mr. Landeau's fingers tattooed the desk—dare be so rash and righteous if she didn't have Chris?

Mr. Landeau snatched the arrow from the air. "Then you may consider your employment with Wintergreen Credit Counseling terminated as of today." He hesitated and finally added reluctantly, "You will, of course, receive salary for the vacation time you have earned to this point."

Silver managed to say, "Thank you."

Stiffly he added, "If you could see your way clear to accommodate the needs of this office by changing your vacation time, I would be willing to reconsider your termination."

Silver hesitated for a split moment, surprised by the conciliatory statement. Then she recognized the offer for what it was, not generosity or a genuine desire that she continue working there, but simply protection for himself should she make some formal complaint about his actions.

"No, thank you."

Silver still had the feeling that she'd plunged headlong into a trap he'd laid for her, although she did have the consolation that he hadn't dared try to cheat her out of the vacation pay. But his "victory" was okay, she reminded herself as she marched back to her cubicle. She'd wanted to get away from Wintergreen, and now she had no choice but to do exactly that. Chris had rammed into his roadblock wall with the Golden Lighthouse deal to change his path; she had her shove from Mr. Landeau to get her going. She would simply trust in the Lord to guide her and open the way.

They talked to the minister at Chris's church and arranged a simple ceremony in a small room adjoining the main sanctuary. They decided to wait until a later date, when time wasn't so cramped, to hold a reception for more relatives and friends. Silver called her parents, brothers, and sister, who delightedly said they'd attend the ceremony. Chris called his brother, but Carol was having some problems with her pregnancy, and though the problems were relatively minor, the doctor advised against travel.

Colleen, even as she was protesting that Silver and Chris couldn't possibly rush home from summer camp on Saturday and get married on Sunday, agreed to be Silver's lone attendant for the ceremony. Chris asked his lawyer friend Dick to be best man. Chris again vetoed Silver's tentative suggestion to include

Ben. After some internal discussion with herself, Silver finally called the other Silver to tell her about the marriage, and she sounded sincere when she said she'd be happy to come to the reception later.

Silver and Chris got their blood tests and marriage license on a couple of his hurried lunch hours. He presented her with a gorgeous marquise diamond flanked by four smaller stones in a dramatic gold setting, and on a Saturday, before a bike ride, they chose matching wedding bands. She bought a softly tailored white suit for the ceremony, and a silk shell in pale orchid and new white heels to wear with it.

They decided on a backpacking expedition in Costa Rica for the honeymoon, a choice that appalled Colleen, who dropped by after work one afternoon to ask Silver's advice on one of Silver's clients who had been reassigned to her.

"A honeymoon should be lazy and luxurious and romantic. Not tromping around by day, eating out of a tin can, and battling bugs by night!"

"Romance," Silver declared grandly if not necessarily grammatically, "is in the eye of the romancees. We're already planning to celebrate our first anniversary with a white-water raft trip in Idaho."

Colleen shook her head and laughed. "You two are suited for each other. Not for anyone else on earth, I suspect, but definitely for each other."

Which was exactly the way it should be, Silver thought with complete satisfaction.

Silver sent out application letters and résumés, contacting both Christian counseling organizations and a network of individuals whom she thought could be helpful. Sometimes she felt a little panicky about the bridge she'd burned behind her at Wintergreen, but she kept repeating the encouraging phrase *crisis is opportunity.*

With the comforting little cushion of thought underneath that, as Chris had pointed out, she wasn't going to be sitting on a street corner with her furniture if she didn't find another job immediately. The only thing she really regretted was knowing that some of her clients at Wintergreen probably felt abandoned.

She had another letter from the auto-parts company, this one grumbling about the "unfairness" of the "antagonism" she had stirred up against them. She told Chris about it on their way to a final meeting of the summer-camp staff. This was Thursday evening, and they'd be leaving for the island on Saturday morning.

"But they aren't willing to do anything about changing the billboard?" he asked.

"They do rather grudgingly say that because of the 'adverse reaction' they won't renew their lease on the billboard at the end of this six-month period."

"So your campaign was, in the long run, a victory."

"I suppose. But until the end of the six months, we'll be seeing overexposed cleavage to advertise auto parts."

"Perhaps not."

His tone was thoughtful, and Silver glanced at him with interest.

"That would be a good billboard location to announce the opening of our new motel. Perhaps, for a suitable fee, they could be persuaded to transfer the remainder of the lease to us."

"Chris, you'd do that? Fantastic!" She scooted across the seat of the pickup and planted an enthusiastic kiss of reward on his cheek.

"I'll check on it tomorrow and let you know what I find out." He tilted his cheek for more rewards and was not disappointed.

As it turned out, however, their conversation the following day was on a much different subject.

Twenty

Jeans, shorts, sweatshirts for cool mornings, short-sleeved tops for warm afternoons. Underthings, extra shoes, socks, swimsuit. Towels, soap, toothbrush, makeup. Bible, pens, notebook. With departure time for the summer camp less than twenty-four hours away, Silver was finally beginning to feel a going-away excitement that, with all the upheaval in her life, had been missing earlier.

But it was an excitement that paled beneath the shivery knowledge that in a little over a week she'd be leaving for Costa Rica with Chris. And married. Married!

But, first things first.

She surveyed the already overflowing duffel bag standing beside her sleeping bag. Did she have everything? No. Pillow! Last year she'd forgotten the pillow and spent the week with her head on various lumpy piles of clothing and towels. She was just adding the pillow and an extra jacket to the pile when the ring of the doorbell surprised her. She peered out the window before opening the door.

"Chris! What are you doing here in the middle of the morning?" He kissed her, but it was a quick, distracted kiss that instantly alerted her. "Is something wrong?"

He stepped around her overstuffed duffel bag. "Well, no, not really. Just a change in plans that I wanted to tell you about in person." He smiled brightly and gave his burgundy tie a yank, as if it felt a little tight. "Good news, actually."

The uncharacteristic phoniness of the smile would do credit to a con man selling fake stocks and bonds. She skipped over the "good news" pitch and headed straight for the fine print. "What kind of 'change in plans'?"

"As you may remember, when the Golden Lighthouse heirs backed out of the deal, they appointed a grandson as general manager of the chain." He lifted a dark eyebrow, and she nodded. "It seems that the grandson instantly started playing Mighty Motel Mogul on a grand scale. Throwing parties with caviar and hundred-dollars-a-bottle champagne, all charged to the company. Outfitting a girlfriend with a new wardrobe from Paris, again with company money. Buying himself a Jaguar."

"And all this changes your plans?"

He perched on the arm of the sofa and tried to draw her into his arms. She smoothly busied herself tying the drawstring on the upright duffel bag. He planted his hands on his thighs and slapped his palms lightly against his blue slacks.

"Because they're reopening the deal to sell the Golden Lighthouse chain."

"I see." Silver straightened slowly. "And you're saying that you have to cancel your commitment to the summer camp so you can be here to negotiate with them." She started to ask, *And what about our wedding?* but deliberately clamped her jaw shut instead.

"Sil, I have to pounce on this now." He jumped up from the arm of the sofa. "The heirs are furious with the grandson, afraid he's going to run the company into the ground, and they're hot to sell now. And this time there's a new complication. Another investor is interested in buying. They're going to play us against each other, of course, and I have to be right here on the spot to keep in the game. Or else the other investor will steal it out from under me."

"I thought you were out of the 'game,' that the roadblock the Lord set in your way showed you a different path you should take instead of continuing this never-ending assault on success!"

"It isn't some fanatic 'assault,' like you make it sound! It's simply a chance I can't let zip right by me. No shrewd business-man could! Can't you see that?" He paced the floor as she so recently had done, frustration in every line of his body. Frustration with her. He didn't give her time to answer before stopping and demanding, "You're saying I should throw all this away just to spend a week at the summer camp?"

"You made a commitment. They may be short-handed with-out you. They…we're counting on you."

"Look, if it's that important, I'll hire a professional lifeguard to take my place." He stopped short, an oh-I-understand-now expression replacing his scowl. "You think I'm backing out on the wedding, too, don't you? Well, I'm not! No way." He kneed the duffel bag aside. "This will all be wrapped up before the end of the week."

"This sounds like a replay of a song I've already heard. And I didn't care all that much for it the first time around!"

"No. It's different this time."

"Is it, Chris? Have possessions and material wealth suddenly become all that important to you? Do you suddenly crave champagne and caviar parties and a Jaguar?"

"No, of course not," he cut in impatiently. "It's—"

Their eyes locked, and he swallowed roughly.

"It's still Ben, isn't it?" she asked softly. "You can't let go of that desperate need to prove something to him."

"It's not just for me. It's for my father, too. He wasn't the worthless, irresponsible, head-in-the-clouds dreamer that Ben has always made him out to be."

"And you think acquiring this other chain of motels, doubling the size of what you now own, will finally prove something to Ben?"

"It might," he growled. "Yes, I think it will. This time I think it will. And Ben is old and not in good mental or physical health. I want to do it before it's too late." He shoved his shirtsleeve back and looked at his watch. "Look, I've got to go. I have a meeting in twenty minutes. But I'll come over this evening, and we'll hash this out."

"Think you can spare the time?" she flared recklessly.

He ignored the taunt. "I will be here even if it's midnight before I make it. And unless you want a shoulder shoving your door in, you'd better be here to open it. Because we are going to talk about this. I love you, Silver. We have to work this out."

She hesitated, frustrated and angry with him, but she couldn't withhold the words. "I love you, too," she finally whispered.

But somehow, Silver thought bleakly, the words from both of them sounded more like desperate pleas than happily-ever-after promises.

She spent the remainder of the morning in a flurry of busy physical activity. Scrubbing the bathroom, cleaning out the overflowing junk drawer in the kitchen, going out for a quick run. But by lunchtime she faced the fact that physical activity was a dead end. What she really needed was thought and prayer time. And by the time Chris returned about nine-thirty that evening, she had something different to say to him.

He was still in the same blue slacks and white shirt he'd

been wearing that morning, although now the burgundy tie was gone, the sleeves of the shirt rolled back, and the collar unbuttoned. His smile was still a little too bright, but his kiss was confident.

"Coffee?" she asked.

He sat on the arm of the sofa again. "No, thanks. I'm already floating in it. I just got out of a meeting with the Golden Lighthouse people, and I'm pretty sure we can wrap this up by Monday or Tuesday. So I'll come out to the camp just as soon as I can get away."

"And if it turns out you can't get away?" She was near tears that he was doing this again, just as he had on her parents' anniversary celebration.

"Sil, I think you should take a more logical, less emotional, look at this."

"And I think you should take a long, hard look at yourself and your life and Ben. Chris, you are a financial success. If Ben can't see, or admit, that now, he never will."

"You can't be sure of that."

"Okay, let's say you make this fantastic deal, and he still isn't convinced. Or, conversely, let's say it falls through again, so you still have nothing with which to convince him. What then?" She answered the question for him. "You keep trying, of course. You simply ignore the Lord's roadblock or try to detour or climb over it."

"It could be that he's removing the roadblock."

She clenched her hands, trying not to let frustration lead her astray in some wild outburst. "Chris, I don't think you're ever going to be able to set aside trying to prove something to Ben or give up your frantic climb for the top, even if that climb is coming between you and the Lord, because there's something else involved here."

"Which is?"

"Forgiveness."

He looked blank.

"You've never been able to forgive Ben. If you could forgive him, you could let all this go. You wouldn't have to prove anything to him. But without forgiveness you're caught like a squirrel in a cage, going round and round, with no way out. Until you settle this between you and Ben and the Lord, you'll be stuck trying to build an empire that will never be enough."

"Forgiveness has nothing to do with it! Ben took me in, raised both me and Brian, provided generously for our needs. He even gave me my start in the motel business! I just want to show him."

"And he's hurt you, hurt you deeply, by running down your father, by dishonoring and disparaging, even vilifying, his memory. For doing the same to you and your beliefs. And he's still doing it. I know he's wrong. He made me furious enough to want to pick up a chair and throw it at him! But, until you can forgive him for what he's done and how he is, I don't think you're ever going to find the real fulfillment that God wants for you. He, through Christ, has forgiven your sins. Can't you forgive, too?"

"Forgiveness has nothing to do with my relationship with Ben," Chris repeated tightly. "I'm capable of forgiving if the situation requires it. It took me a long time, and for a while it felt as if I were betraying my parents by doing it, but I managed to forgive their murderers."

"Yes, I know you did! And it must have been like…cutting your heart out."

"And serving it up for brunch."

"Then, if you could do that—"

"But with Ben, forgiveness is…irrelevant. It's simply a matter of making him see and acknowledge the facts. The truth. Ben sure doesn't see himself as needing forgiveness. Some big expression of forgiveness from me would be meaningless and irrelevant, maybe even infuriating, to him."

"But not to God. And not to you, although that may be difficult to see now."

"Ben isn't forgiving toward my father!"

"I know. But sometimes forgiving has to be one-sided."

He merely slashed the air with an impatient gesture of his arm, a gesture so negative that Silver shook her head and dropped to the chair opposite the sofa in defeat.

"Look," he began, his tone determinedly softer and conciliatory. "We'll work this out."

"No, Chris, I don't think we will. I don't think I can marry a man who's always going to put this frantic climb to financial success ahead of everything else. Ahead of serving the Lord, ahead of me."

"You're breaking our engagement just because you think it's possible the honeymoon to Costa Rica could be delayed a day or two?" he challenged scornfully.

Breaking our engagement.

Was that what she was doing?

She swallowed, looking down to find she was twisting the diamond on her left hand as if it were burning her finger. It glowed with a dazzling radiance in the lamplight. Yes, now that he mentioned it, the fact that the honeymoon might be pushed back while he worked on the big business deal did matter. But she could live with that if she thought it was a one-time thing. But it wasn't. Not one time with her, not one time with the Lord.

She lifted her gaze to his. *Oh, Chris, I love you....*

But this would never work.

She rose to her feet. She gave the ring another harsh twist. It came off in her hand. She thrust it at him. For a moment he looked as if he were simply going to let the ring fall to the floor, but finally he grabbed it, jammed it in his pocket, and stalked to the door.

She just stood there after the door closed behind him. She knew she was going to cry, and yet at that moment, the shock blocked even tears. She looked at her pile of camp supplies stacked by the sofa. She studied her watch, the circle of numbers oddly meaningless. Numbly she realized she should get some sleep. She had to be at the church at five-thirty tomorrow morning. She had to be in shape to cope with a crowd of noisy, energetic kids for a week.

But instead she just dropped to a cross-legged position on the floor and sat there, shoulders slumped. The tears came finally, the sorrow, the regret, the pain. The anger that rose in explosion but melted back into pain. She rubbed the empty space on her finger where the ring had been. She mentally touched the gaping wound in her heart. She looked to a future that had once shimmered with sunlight but was now misted in fog.

Yet, eventually, sometime in the depths of the night, thoughts surfaced through the pain. Panicky, practical thoughts. She wasn't going to be Mrs. Chris Bentley. She was out of a job. She had no current prospects for finding one anytime soon.

Crisis is opportunity, she'd claimed to both Chris and herself. Follow the path the Lord wants you to take.

But not easy to do when you were out on a limb, with a chain saw buzzing beside you and panic rising within.

Especially when there was a simple way to stop that buzzing chain saw. Mr. Landeau had grudgingly offered to let her keep the job if she gave in on the vacation-time disagreement. She could go to the church tomorrow morning, tell Hank she couldn't make summer camp after all, contact Mr. Landeau at home with meek apologies.

Or she could trust in the Lord, trust that he was going to help her find opportunity in this crisis.

Twenty-one

She sent her fears to the Lord in prayer and resolutely tackled her problems.

First, even though the hurt was foremost in her thoughts and emotions, there was the mundane matter of a wedding to cancel, people to notify. It would be difficult to do from the island, and by the time she got home from camp, it would be too late. So she found herself in the incongruous position of calling people at four-thirty in the morning to notify them that the wedding was off. First her parents, her father's first reaction panicky at the odd-hour phone call, then bewildered and sympathetic. Then her sister, who, always there for her in a true emergency, offered to come over instantly if Silver needed her. Silver thanked her and said she'd be fine. Then Colleen, and finally, the other Silver. She really didn't have to call the other Silver, but she did, knowing that this woman, probably better than anyone, would understand. She was right.

The other Silver asked a one-word question after she heard the news. "Work?"

"Bingo." Silver swallowed. "I'll tell you more later."

She arrived at the church ten minutes early, but at the last minute, rather than riding in one of the two big converted school buses being used to transport kids and staff, she wound up deciding to drive her own car to Anacortes, where they would catch a ferry to the islands. Technically this was because Hank Arlands needed someone to run out to the home of one of the girls and pick up some forgotten medicine, but she also jumped on the chance because of a sneaky little awareness that she *could*, if her presence at camp didn't seem absolutely vital, return home Sunday evening and on Monday morning make a plea to Mr. Landeau for the return of her job.

In spite of the stormy scene in her apartment, she couldn't help peering hopefully at each arriving car as she helped load kids and camping gear into the buses. Perhaps Chris would change his mind.

But no rough pickup swung into the parking lot. No familiar, dark-haired figure rushed to the bus. She watched the buses pull out, not realizing until a parent politely asked, "Did you hurt your hand?" that she was rubbing her naked finger as if it were on fire.

She detoured to pick up the medicine and reached the ferry landing in Anacortes, some seventy-five miles north of Seattle, just as the buses were being loaded into the yawning mouth of the ferry. She hastily parked her car, bought a ticket, and boarded the ferry seconds before the gate closed. She stood with arms braced on the railing, watching the ferry churn away from the dock in a boil of white water, her throat tight as she thought how she'd expected to be sharing this with Chris. Then she determinedly cast that aside and went to find her group of campers and staff. A bank of clouds lingered on the western horizon, but the sky above was gloriously blue, the brisk wind that tossed her hair invigorating. Who needed Chris Bentley? she asked herself, not for the first time.

The logistics of getting everyone to the island were not simple. The ferry route touched at only four of the numerous San Juan Islands, and the small island where their camp was located was not one of them. They had to unload the buses on Lopez Island, drive across the island to a forest-ringed bay where Hank had several motorboats waiting, and then transport individual small groups across open water to the island.

Silver rounded up the six girls assigned to her tent, but her group was among the last to make the crossing. By that time the water had roughened considerably, and the girls shrieked and squealed with each *wham-wham-wham* of the bow hitting the white-capped waves. One girl, Pam, with long blond hair and a sulky mouth, abruptly became sick, and the boat had to stop while she hung her head over the stern.

"I didn't want to come to this dumb camp anyway, but my mom made me so that she could go to Reno with her boyfriend," Pam muttered resentfully when she finally lifted her head and wiped her mouth with the tissue Silver handed her. "I hate campfires and sleeping on the ground and praying and boring stories about Jesus. And I think I'm going to be sick the whole time I'm here," she added in what sounded more like satisfaction than fear.

"Yuck." Alisha wrinkled her freckled nose. "If you're going to throw up, I don't want to be in the same tent with you."

"Is there a McDonald's?" a third girl named Tammy asked. She peered suspiciously at the green island ahead, as if they were advancing on some savage outpost beyond civilization. "Or a place to rent videos?"

Silver had to admit, if you considered a McDonald's the standard by which to judge the level of civilization, that they probably were headed for a week on its outer limits. Which for her was one of the major appeals of the island camp, of course.

Silver explained to the girls, while the boat bobbed in the water as they waited to see if Pam's stomach was going to overflow again, that although the island had no McDonald's, no video rentals, no store of any kind, there were lots of fun things to do. Hiking, swimming, games, and yes, with a pointed look at Pam, learning about Jesus. The twenty-five-acre estate belonging to the wealthy man who provided the camp took up more than half of the small island. A primitive airstrip separated the estate from a handful of homes on the far side of the island, places that were not even visible from the camp.

Alisha responded to this information with what was apparently her all-purpose comment. "Yuck. And don't take my picture," she snapped at a small, dark-haired girl named Karine who had been industriously clicking her camera ever since they got on the boat.

Oh, this is going to be a fun week, Silver groaned silently. Hank usually mixed girls he knew to be strong believers and who had been at camp before with new girls. But this year they had an excess of older, new girls, and Silver, as an experienced counselor theoretically able to cope, had drawn a full tent of them.

The situation did not improve when they reached land.

"This tent *smells*," Pam stated with an exaggerated wrinkle of her nose as Silver supervised staking of the corners in their assigned spot.

The tent also didn't go up the way it should. A metal rod was supposed to go through a long nylon tube, and it stubbornly refused to budge.

Pam, little interested in Silver's struggles, glanced up at the estate owner's magnificent hillside house, built just above a spectacular cliff that dropped in jagged outcroppings directly to the sea. "Why can't we stay up there?"

"Because this is the area the owner provides for us," Silver said with more patience than she felt. Seeing Pam still eyeing the big house with a certain air of speculation, she added, "In fact, we are specifically not allowed in that private area."

"Is the owner here now?"

"I don't think so. He lives in Seattle, and his health isn't good. Although he comes out a few times a year, I think."

"That's pretty stingy, if he isn't even here and we still can't use it." Pam grumbled. "I'll bet it's really nice."

"I'd say the owner is exceedingly generous in allowing us to use his property at all, and we should be grateful to him," Silver returned, unable to keep the exasperation out of her voice.

Pam's only response was a surly look and an equally surly kick to tumble her duffel bag in the general direction of the tent. Karine snapped a photo, earning her a glare from Pam and giggles from two other girls, Kim and Sandra.

These girls were not Silver's particular responsibility during the day, but she tried to keep an eye on them anyway. Swimming and outdoor games were scheduled for that afternoon, but the wind was blowing so hard that all but the most boisterous kids stayed under the open-sided cookhouse shelter, playing games or simply milling around. A few sprinkles marred the evening campfire, but at least by then the wind wasn't threatening to rip tent stakes out of the ground. Silver talked to Hank for a minute before heading for her tent.

"Did you find someone to take Chris's tent?" Because she had introduced Chris to Hank and helped arrange his participation here, she felt responsible for the gap left when he backed out.

"We've split his assigned boys among other tents until he gets here, although we really need him as a lifeguard. But he said on the phone that he'd join us as soon as he could get some important business problem taken care of."

"Don't count on it," Silver muttered under her breath.

Later, inside the tent, Silver tried to get the girls talking and sharing about themselves. She got a few shy statements out of Karine about her interest in photography, but Pam, who was a year older than most of the girls because of some school problems, and definitely more sophisticated, had managed to establish herself as leader, and when she said scornfully, "I'm going to bed," the other girls followed. Silver woke to the steady drum of rain on the tent at twelve-thirty-five, according to her glow-in-the-dark clock. The first yelp about leaks came at twelve-thirty-six.

"Hey! I'm getting dripped on!"

"So am I!"

"I don't see how the tent could be leaking. We checked all these tents thoroughly." Silver found a flashlight and crawled around on her hands and knees. She couldn't find any leaks, although there were definitely drops of water on the sleeping bags and the faces of the two girls.

There was another leak alarm an hour later. Then Tammy had to go to the rest room. Silver went with her. When they returned wet and cold and Silver slid into her sleeping bag, the midsection felt as clammy as damp laundry. She spent the remainder of the night trying to avoid the soggy spot.

By morning, rain still hammered the camp. Sunday services, planned for the open meadow, were held under the drafty shelter instead. By afternoon several tents had to be moved out of low areas. Mud clumped on shoes and encouraged slips and slides. One set of rest rooms clogged up, leaving long lines at the others. The evening campfire smoldered sullenly instead of dancing with cheery flames.

Monday was no improvement. The big gas stove in the kitchen shut down on one side, cutting the cooking area in half. The only good thing about the situation that Silver could see was that Chris's talents as a lifeguard were not missed. No one wanted to go near the cold, rough water. All the problems also kept Silver from thinking too much about Chris. Although all too often she found herself absentmindedly touching that empty ring finger. And later that day she discovered the source of the "leaks" in the tent.

Just before dinner she herded a reluctant Pam to a secluded nook behind the cooking area in the shelter and told her that she'd found the plastic bottle and straw Pam had used to dribble water on her companions in the night as well as dampen Silver's own sleeping bag.

"I didn't do that!" Pam denied hotly. "I need water because I get thirsty at night. I have this…uh…throat problem." She clutched her throat melodramatically, but changing tactics like a football player dodging a tackle, she added indignantly, "Besides, what're you doing digging around in my private stuff anyway?"

"I wasn't digging. I was looking for those so-called leaks in the tent, and I accidentally squashed your plastic bottle with my knee. *Your* bed now has a big wet spot in it."

"Well, thanks a lot! At least I didn't dump the whole bottle in your—" Pam shrugged, dismissing her own incriminating statement as if continuing to deny her guilt were too much bother. "Okay, so what? It's boring here. What happens now? I get nailed to a cross or something?"

"Oh, Pam." Silver shook her head, feeling oddly helpless at the girl's determined stubbornness not to hear what was being taught here and feeling hurt that the girl could so carelessly trivialize the sacrifice Jesus had made. "Sins of his own weren't why Jesus was nailed to the cross. He went to the cross for *our* sins, yours and mine."

If she thought Pam would suddenly see the light, she was wrong.

"Big deal," Pam muttered. "You probably never committed a single sin in your whole life anyway. Why should you?

Everything's perfect for you. You're beautiful and smart, and everyone likes you, and no one runs off and leaves you. You even have a pretty name, like a movie star."

Silver shook her head again, hardly knowing where to attack that strange lineup. "Pam, I'm not perfect, and I need forgiveness too, and bad things do happen in my life. I got fired from my job a couple of weeks ago, and I don't know when I'll find another one. Just the night before we came out here my fiancé and I broke up, and I spent most of the night crying."

Pam's usually sullen eyes momentarily flickered with interest, but then she shrugged. "You'll find another one. My mom always does."

Silver didn't know whether that unfeeling statement applied to jobs or boyfriends, but impulsively she asked, "Pam, do you really hate being here? Or is what you hate more that your mom went off without you to have fun?"

Pam rolled her eyes. "Now you sound like that shrink she sent me to."

The dinner bell gonged then, and Pam raced off to join the little coterie of followers she'd gathered around her, leaving Silver to her frustration. Although the thought occurred to her that this conversation with Pam was almost the first time she'd thought about her lack of a job; leaving camp and scurrying back to Landeau to try to reclaim her position at Wintergreen hadn't even entered her mind since camp had begun. She was, though her gait might be a bit wobbly, walking with the Lord in trust.

One thing changed that night, however. After the steady deluge of rain, the tent actually started leaking. Silver woke in the morning to find a puddle of water beside her sleeping bag. While Silver was sopping it up with towels, Pam complained bitterly that her new sandals were wet and ruined; Alisha said, "Yuck," at least fourteen times; Tammy caught her pajamas in the zipper of the sleeping bag; and Karine and the other two girls all had the sniffles. At breakfast that morning murmurs and rumors about giving up and closing camp early flew from table to table.

But just after a soggy lunch, a rift appeared in the gloomy cloud cover. A sliver of blue peeked through. Everyone stood around watching with the kind of interest usually reserved for a fast-action video game. The rift slowly widened to a definite crack and then a ragged circle. And through that open circle came an unexpected sight.

Twenty-two

The helicopter slowly settled to earth, whirling blades stirring tall grass at the edge of the rough airstrip. The door of the bubble cockpit opened, and Chris swung to the ground, duffel bag tucked under one arm. He ducked as he ran to the fence before the helicopter lifted off in a silvery flash of spinning blades. It all happened so quickly that Silver couldn't help blinking in astonishment.

"Wow, is that the guy who owns this place?" Pam asked "I thought he'd be old and decrepit."

"No, that's just one of the counselors arriving late."

There was definitely nothing old and decrepit about Chris as he vaulted the fence and strode toward camp. He wore faded jeans, a denim jacket, a red-plaid shirt, and a neon red baseball cap. The kids, impressed with this dramatic arrival, swarmed toward him. He met them with a big, conquering-hero grin. Hank Arlands clapped Chris on the shoulder as if he were some long-lost buddy rather than a self-centered man who had put storming the bastions of business success ahead of commitment to the Lord's service.

Silver did not join the throng asking excited questions. She just leaned against one of the square wooden posts supporting the shelter, arms crossed. Chris hesitated as he passed her, as if he might say something, but the boys who'd originally been assigned to his tent were clamoring for his attention and vying for the privilege of carrying his duffel bag. Silver returned his nod of greeting with a bare jerk of her chin.

From the looks of that grin, she thought as she turned back to the kitchen-cleanup duties assigned to her this day, he'd obviously aced out the competition and pulled off the coup of his career. At the moment she was too annoyed and angry to care if he'd finally managed to impress Ben with his big deal for the Golden Lighthouse chain. *We'll just see how long that grin holds up when you're up to your ankles in mud, water is rising like a tidal wave around your sleeping bag, and the kids are threatening to make* Mutiny on the Bounty *look like a friendly afternoon sail,* she thought sourly.

But that didn't happen. She didn't want to feel *dismay*…after all, she wanted summer camp to be a rewarding and happy experience for the kids. Yet she couldn't help feeling grumpy that, almost as if the blades of that helicopter had been some high-tech magic wand, everything changed when Chris arrived. No deluge of rain for Chris. No wondering if mold was starting to grow between *his* toes. No one ominously muttering to him, "If I catch something awful here, my mom will sue you."

The change started instantly. The helicopter had no more than exited through the rough circle in the clouds than the blue space widened and expanded to cover a quarter of the sky, then half. Sunshine blazed through. The ground steamed. Heavy jackets came off. Spirits lifted. The men rigged lines to hang clothes and sleeping bags out to dry.

Chris's tent went up like a mushroom sprouting after a rain, with none of the frustrating struggles she'd experienced erecting her tent. His assigned boys were cheerful and helpful. The two men who had been working on the clogged lines at the rest room unexpectedly reported success. An informal soccer game started. Basketballs dropped through the hoop fastened at the end of the shelter. Frisbees swooped and flew. One of the cooks accidentally dropped a big pot on the cookstove, and the stove miraculously came out of its sulk and started working again.

A few people had known about the relationship between Silver and Chris, but she'd told Hank that it was over. He'd apparently passed the word along, and no one asked questions or offered unwanted sympathy. Silver didn't want to talk to Chris, yet she also found herself perversely annoyed that he made no special effort to talk to her. He was busy every minute, always surrounded by an eager entourage.

That night's campfire was the first one that could be called successful. The fire crackled cheerfully. The kids sang with lusty enthusiasm. Chris told his bear-and-pillow story. Everyone trooped off to their tents with friendly calls rather than snarls and grumbles.

Silver detoured to the shelter to drop her coffee cup in the deep metal sink before going to her tent for the night. She almost collided with Chris as she rounded one of the wooden tables with attached benches. She stepped back hastily, uncertain whether this meeting was planned or a surprise to him as well as to her.

He caught her by the upper arms. "You've been avoiding me," he accused without preliminaries.

Her arms, like the instinctive jerk of a leg in response to a tap on the knee, almost went around his neck, as though, disconnected from her angry emotions, that was where they *wanted* to go. She stopped them and flung his arms aside. "I've been busy. I take my responsibilities and duties here seriously." The unspoken words *unlike some people* crackled like an arc of electricity between them. "I assume congratulations are in order?"

His head tilted thoughtfully in the harsh light of the bulb left burning all night in the shelter. "Yes, I think perhaps they are."

"Have you talked to Ben?"

"Yes."

"Was he impressed?"

Chris shrugged lightly. "You know Ben." He hesitated. Night bugs dancing around the bulb cast little flickering shadows across his face. "So now what?"

"Now what about what?" she responded.

"About us."

"We've already discussed *us*. Nothing's changed."

"I'm here."

"You said you'd be here as soon as you got the deal wrapped up, probably Monday or Tuesday. So now it's Tuesday, and here you are, right on schedule. Now, if you'll excuse me, I have to get to my tent. My girls tend to think up little surprises for me if I'm not on guard." She was reasonably certain the grasshopper in her sleeping bag last night had not gotten there without some assistance from Pam.

"Silver, this isn't exactly what you think."

Some agitation in his tone made her pause a step beyond the shelter. Was she mistaken? He'd turned away from the light, and his face was in shadows as she peered at him. "The deal didn't fall through again, did it?"

"No. But—"

"Then enjoy your summer camp. See you around."

She marched off toward her tent, the dignity of her rigid-backed exit only slightly marred by the plunge of her right foot into a muddy puddle.

The next day was as glorious as the earlier ones had been miserable. For the first time they could conduct morning classes in spacious, open sunlight instead of being cramped under the shelter. Water around the island never really warmed above an icy level, but the day was so warm and sunny that almost everyone donned swimsuits and headed for the sandy beach.

Silver watched Chris, looking, in his swim trunks, all too much like some star on a Hunks of the Year calendar, help set up the roped floats that marked the swimming area. He then performed his lifeguard duties with admirable diligence, even rushing in once to herd Pam and another girl back into the designated area with a masculine authority that brought none of the back talk Silver usually got from Pam.

That morning, when Silver had chided Pam for the messiness of her area of the tent, Pam had merely taunted, "Oh, are you going to send me home as punishment? Good!" Then she'd deliberately widened her eyes and slapped her own cheek in a phony gesture of suddenly remembering something. "Oh, but you can't do that, can you? Because there's no one there to send me home to!" Silver had already passed the word along to other counselors to offer special prayers for this troubled, and troublesome, girl.

The counselors rotated from table to table at meals, so campers and staff members would all have some exposure to each other over the course of the week, and at dinner that evening Silver found herself at the table next to Chris's. In fact, if either of them leaned back, their backs would have touched across the narrow aisle. She stiffly took care *not* to lean back and carefully ignored him, although he was so busy talking and laughing with the kids at the table that she doubted he even knew he was being ignored.

Halfway through the meal a thought occurred to her, something she really should mention to Chris. She waited until he gathered his dishes and lifted a long leg over the bench.

She turned, as if she'd only then noticed him. "Do you have a minute?" she asked in a polite, formal tone.

"Sure. You kids take your dishes on over to the tray, and scrape 'em *clean,*" he called to his group. "I'll be out to shoot some baskets with you in a minute." He sat down again, straddling the bench, and turned his attention to Silver.

"I was just thinking.... I notified my family and Colleen that the wedding was canceled, but I wondered if you'd thought to tell the minister that he wouldn't be needed Sunday afternoon."

"No, actually I didn't. I guess it slipped my mind."

Silver clenched her fists at that careless, cavalier remark, which relegated cancellation of the wedding to the insignificance of calling off an appointment with someone trying to sell you insurance. Stiffly she said, "He is, after all, the pastor of your church, so I think it would be most appropriate if you did it."

"I'll take care of it when I get home."

Just then Hank Arlands came by and paused at Chris's empty table. "Hey, before I forget it, some guys from church are getting together for a men's breakfast next Thursday. Would you like to join us?"

"I'd like to, but I'll be backpacking in Costa Rica next week," Chris said without so much as a glance at Silver.

"That sounds great! Some kind of a club or group outing?" Hank asked.

"No, just me."

Silver indignantly grabbed her dishes and silverware and headed for the tray, uncertain whether to laugh or cry. Chris was blithely going on *their* honeymoon, apparently unconcerned that she wouldn't be along! She'd been much too kind when she once called him an insensitive clod, she fumed. She was still searching for a more appropriate term of censure and condemnation as she lay sleepless, listening to the lap of waves on the beach that night. Was Chris listening to them too, also unable to sleep?

No. He was undoubtedly dreaming happily about his vast new motel empire. Or a carefree week of solo backpacking in Costa Rica.

A planned part of each evening was that any camper who wanted to make a commitment to Christ, or simply have a time for special counseling or prayer, was invited to stay after the general dismissal from the campfire. The following evening Tammy surprised Silver by staying, and when she came to the tent later, she was quietly bubbling with happiness and said she'd given her heart to Jesus. Silver hugged her, and during the brief, before-bedtime devotionals, she gave special thanks to the Lord for this blessing.

Pam, of course, simply sat there looking bored and scornful, her Bible carelessly flung open to the wrong place. Immediately after the prayer she jumped up and said she had to go to the rest room.

"Are you ill?" Silver asked, remembering the warning issued on the boat trip. "I can go with you."

"I'm not some baby who has to have her hand held to go to the bathroom," Pam said scornfully. "C'mon, Karine, let's go."

Karine obediently jumped up to follow. It certainly wasn't camp policy to restrict trips to the rest rooms, but Silver watched the two duck out of the tent with a certain uneasiness. This was an alliance that troubled her because she feared Pam's influence on the small, shy girl. Yet in spite of her frustration and occasional anger with Pam, she could also see the hurting little girl inside. She wouldn't put some late-night escapade past Pam, but the two were back within five minutes, Pam's glance insolently saying she knew Silver had been worrying. Which, Silver suspected in frustration, was probably the main reason Pam had made the trip.

The weather remained glorious, and by now the miserable first days had taken on mythical proportions, the kind of thing about which fond stories would be told in years to come.

But on Friday morning, as Silver was helping with an arts and crafts class, a shrill scream of panic pierced the usual hum of camp activity.

Twenty-three

Silver didn't recognize the scream, but she recognized the long blond hair streaming behind the figure racing across the meadow. She dropped the pinecone doll she was helping a little girl make and ran toward Pam. The scream was a recognizable word now.

"Help! Help! *Help!*"

A couple of male counselors got to the girl first, Chris one of them. Silver ran up as Chris steadied the girl with an arm around her shoulders. Pam was so out of breath that her panted words were unintelligible, but she flung her arm toward the hillside. There, on the jagged cliff below the big house, a dot of white clung to the rocks.

"Karine!" Pam gasped. "Karine...*fell!*"

Hank, who'd just arrived, didn't ask for explanations of how it happened or what the girls were doing in this off-limits area. He simply snapped orders for rope and the stretcher that was part of their basic medical supplies and with a rapid-fire stab of pointed finger picked four men to accompany him and two more to follow with the stretcher. The camp nurse was already running toward the hillside.

"Everyone else, stay here!" Hank commanded. "We don't need a crowd up there causing more accidents."

Silver started to protest. Karine was from her tent. She wanted to help! But she recognized the wisdom of Hank's commands, and she also saw the strange, almost dazed, look of shock on Pam's face, so different from her usual insolence. Impulsively she wrapped her arms around Pam, and together they watched the men follow the nurse disappearing under the trees canopying the road that led up to the house.

It seemed to take hours before the men reappeared near the rail fence bordering the crest of the cliff, although logic told Silver it couldn't have been more than four or five minutes at most. She spotted Chris's neon red baseball cap instantly and followed its movement over the fence and along the precarious edge of the cliff.

Silver didn't ask questions, but suddenly Pam started babbling. "I didn't mean for her to fall! I just wanted to look around the house and see if there was a swimming pool, and I talked Karine into skipping classes and coming with me. And then I climbed out on that point of rock on the other side of the fence to get a better look at camp down here. And she said would I take a picture with her camera from out there, and I told her she was a real weenie if she didn't come out and take it herself. So she did, but she looked down and said she was dizzy…and then she started to wobble and dropped her camera and grabbed for it—" Pam paused and choked on a gulp. "And then she was falling.…"

Silver rocked her gently. "They'll rescue her. See?" She pointed toward the cliff. "They've tied a rope around one of the men, and he's going after her right now."

But Silver spoke with more assurance than she felt because the white dot that was Karine clung so precariously to the jagged cliff. What if she was caught only by a scrap of her shirt, and a bare touch or movement sent her plunging to the sea? She shuddered.

Faint sounds of the men talking to each other floated down from the cliff. The man in the rope sling wasn't Chris. She could see his neon red cap at the top of the cliff, where he was helping to hold the rope, and she breathed a prayer of thanks for his strength.

"But what if she's dead when they get to her?" Pam cried, asking the question Silver hadn't even let herself face. "Dead, and it's my fault!"

"We'll pray for her." She moved the girl toward a prayer group that was already forming a few feet away. "We'll pray for the men to bring her up safely."

The prayers were fervent but brief. No one could stop looking at the life-or-death scene being played out there on the cliff. Someone produced binoculars. Silver focused on Chris when the binoculars reached her. She saw the strain on his face, even the rope cutting into his hands. She moved the binoculars to Karine. The man in the sling was touching her now.... *Don't fall, don't fall!* Silver pleaded in a wild prayer. Yes, he had her.... She was in his arms now! The men slowly drew the pair upward, the man's back grating over the rough rock as he protectively shielded the girl with his body. There, they were at the top, safe—

Silver caught her breath.

No! A length of coiled rope whipped and lashed like a striking snake.... Karine and the man in the sling plunged downward.... Chris lunged toward the falling pair, and she could almost hear his leg crack as it hit the edge of the cliff. But grimly he was pulling, pulling.

And then movement of the other men blocked her view of him, and someone grabbed the binoculars, and all she could do was stand there with eyes straining so intently toward the cliff that the scene dissolved into an out-of-focus blur.

"Did someone else get hurt?" Pam asked in an unnaturally small voice.

Silver tried to swallow, but her throat was too dry. "Yes, I think so."

Silver held firm to obeying Hank's command that everyone stay in camp, until she saw the men carrying the stretcher holding Karine start down the hill, the nurse close beside the injured girl.

But Chris was not with them. Where was he? She strained her eyes for that identifying neon red cap…and found it, halfway down the cliff! But no, it was only the hat, not a body. And now she spotted an inert figure at the crest of the cliff, another man crouched beside it.

She raced across the meadow, meeting the men carrying the stretcher as they emerged from the trees at the base of the hill. Karine's face was scratched and battered, her clothes shredded by the rocks, but she was conscious.

"I'm sorry I went up there, Miss Sinclair," she gulped. She struggled to sit up in the stretcher, and Silver was relieved to see both her arms and legs move even as the nurse gently restrained her. "I know I shouldn't have."

Silver squeezed her hand reassuringly, and in spite of her worries about Chris, she managed to tease Karine lightly. "Lesson learned the hard way?"

"We'll take her down to camp and call for a helicopter, then come back up for Chris," Hank said.

She didn't ask if Chris was hurt. It was obvious. "How bad?" she managed to choke.

Hank hesitated, as if momentarily considering telling her to follow orders and get back to camp, but something in her pleading face apparently made him soften his stance. He simply jerked his head toward the road, giving her silent permission. "I think he'll be okay. But he won't be doing any backpacking in Costa Rica next week."

Silver tore up the steep hill, breathless by the time she climbed over the rail fence. Yet she felt oddly shy and awkward when she knelt beside Chris. She felt an almost painful overflowing of love, even though it didn't change what had ripped their relationship apart. The presence of the other man, an older counselor named Bill, was also constraining. Bill had already taken off his shirt and used it to pillow Chris's head.

"For a Mighty Motel Mogul, you don't look too good," she finally managed to say shakily.

A lump was already forming below his right eye, and his body had an awkward twist, as if he were in pain even as he managed a smile. He held one leg with the knee in a natural bend, but the other leg was oddly flat and straight. His hands, where he'd slid headlong over the cliff, looked as if they'd been scraped with a wire brush. She found a tissue in her pocket and patted at the oozing blood, lowering her head to hide the tears. "I was watching you through binoculars, but I couldn't tell…" her voice faltered. "What happened?"

"I'm not sure. Everything was going fine, and then one of the guys got his foot tangled in the rope coiled behind us, and I grabbed for the sling when it started to slip back down…and here I am."

There was more to it than that. She'd seen him lunge for the rope, recklessly disregarding his own safety. "A hero."

"If so, then a rather clumsy one."

"Are you…hurting?" Instantly she apologized. "I'm sorry. That was a dumb question. I can see you are. Can I do anything?"

For a moment, in spite of the pain, a familiar playful light flickered in his eyes, and she knew if Bill had not been there he'd have teasingly suggested a kiss would help. But all he said was, "My lower leg feels strange. The nurse said it was broken, but...is it still *there?*"

She ran her hands lightly over his denim-clad leg. She was no expert, but even she could identify a crook in a bone that should be straight. "It's still here. Hank is calling for a helicopter to transport you and Karine off the island. So you get to make a dramatic exit as well as a grand entrance."

He made a noise that tried to be a laugh but turned into a teeth-grit of pain as a spasm hit his back. "I guess dramatic exits are my specialty, aren't they?"

"I'm sorry. I shouldn't have said that," she muttered, aware of the double meaning of his comment.

He stayed stiff, back slightly arched, for several more endless seconds until the spasm in the muscle loosened; then his back relaxed again, this time with sweat beading his forehead. Her tissue was already soaked with blood, so she used her shirttail to wipe his forehead.

"They've started back up the hill with the stretcher. They'll be here in just a few minutes to carry you down."

He edged his hand toward her, and she took it. "Sil—" He moistened his lips and swallowed, and she thought he was going to say something vital and momentous. She leaned toward him.

"Yes?"

"When you go home, you might drive around by that billboard. We bought out the auto-parts company's lease, and there should be a new ad on the billboard by now."

She swallowed back a wry disappointment at this mundane announcement. "Thanks. I'll do that." Another spasm hit his back, and she wiped his forehead again. "Maybe it would be better if you didn't try to talk."

He closed his eyes and followed her advice. But he didn't let go of her hand.

~ ~ ~ ~ ~

A helicopter arrived within half an hour, this one especially equipped to handle medical emergencies. They had another stretcher, and both Karine and Chris were loaded on board. Then the helicopter lifted off, within seconds turning into a mere dot in the sky. Silver just stood there, telling herself she was not going to cry.

Which was a little difficult, with tears streaming down her face.

"Miss Sinclair?"

Silver turned, guiltily realizing she'd forgotten all about Pam. She wiped the back of her hand across the tears.

"Are they going to be all right?"

"Yes, I think so."

Pam glanced around uneasily. "Everybody hates me now because it was my fault."

For a moment Silver's emotions flared with hot anger and resentment. Yes, all this was Pam's fault. Her selfish disobedience and callous taunting of shy little Karine had caused all of this!

"I'll bet even Jesus hates me now."

"Oh, Pam—Jesus doesn't hate you! It's human nature to resent someone who causes others harm. But Jesus is always ready to forgive when we accept him into our hearts and ask for forgiveness." With a rush of regret and guilt for her own selfish feelings, she abandoned her anger and resentment and gave the girl an impulsive hug. "I wish you hadn't done what you did."

"So do I! And I'm so sorry. I really am." Tears streamed down Pam's face, too.

"And I don't hate you."

Silver briefly discussed with Hank what Pam had done, an

infraction of rules with consequences so serious that they would probably have sent the girl home if camp were not ending in the morning. Under the circumstances, however, they decided there was really no appropriate disciplinary action that could be taken.

Silver hoped Pam would stay for counseling or prayer after the campfire that evening, when a number did stay to make commitments to Christ on this final night of camp, but Pam slipped away early. Later, when Silver and the other girls crawled into the tent for the night, Pam was already there, curled with her back to them. Although Silver doubted the girl was actually asleep, she kept the bedtime prayers at a whisper level, and she thought she heard a small sob when she asked for the Lord's care and healing for Chris and Karine.

Silver didn't sleep for a long time, either. She thought about Chris…. She thought about love and ambition and Ben and a thin white scar, about a backpacking trip to Costa Rica that would never be.

For the first time, she also thought about moving her job search elsewhere, away from Seattle, maybe across the country. And all the time her fingers went round and round the barren spot where a ring had once been.

Twenty-four

reaking camp the next morning was the usual "planned disorganization," as Hank called it. This time Silver's tent group was among the first across the open water in a motorboat, and they were all very aware of their missing member. Pam didn't get sick, and Tammy said, "You know, I didn't even miss McDonald's," although Alisha still muttered, "Yuck," when she slipped getting out of the boat and got her foot wet. Pam kept to herself, seeming preoccupied, although she occasionally shot Silver odd, secretive little glances.

Silver asked Hank if he knew where the helicopter had taken Chris, and he said Chris had asked to be flown all the way into a Seattle hospital. Where he would be in a better position to run his newly expanded empire from his hospital bed, she thought wryly.

She was standing alone at the rail on the ferry heading back to Anacortes when Pam unexpectedly came up beside her.

"I thought I'd buy Karine a new camera when I got home," Pam said. "Could you get her address for me?"

"I can do that. And I think she'd really appreciate a new camera. That's very nice of you."

Pam tapped nails inexpertly polished in a startling shade of fuchsia on the rail. "Somebody told me something this morning that I didn't know."

Silver smiled but chose not to comment on Pam's generally know-it-all attitude. "And what was that?"

"That the guy got who got hurt rescuing Karine was your boyfriend."

Silver tried not to show surprise that this gossip about her private life had reached the kids. "He was my fiancé, but as I told you, we broke up."

"But you ran all the way up the hill to him! Do you still love him?"

Silver's hands gripped the rail at the blunt question, a question she'd been avoiding. But after a moment's soul-searching, she answered it honestly. "Yes, I guess I do. But sometimes even when there's love, things stand between people."

Pam nodded slowly. "Yeah, like me and my mom sometimes, I guess. But even though you love him, and I was the one who got him hurt, you still don't hate me?"

"I was upset with you," Silver admitted, still tied to honesty. "But no, I don't hate you."

"Really?" Pam still sounded unconvinced.

"Really." She searched for some way to make that plain. "Can you come to our church?"

"No, I live too far away. I only went to camp because somebody told my mom about it, and it came at the right time for her to go to Reno with Rick."

Silver felt a brief anger at this mother, who had helped make her daughter the confused girl she was, but then she concentrated on what she could do to help. "Even if you can't come to church, you and I can still be friends and keep in touch," she said firmly.

"Really?"

"Really. We'll go find a pen and paper and exchange phone numbers and addresses. I'll call you, and you can call me anytime. *Anytime,*" she emphasized.

"You really do forgive me for what I did, don't you?" Pam sounded almost awed.

Silver wrapped an arm around Pam's shoulders and squeezed. "I've made lots of mistakes, too. I forgive you."

"Okay, then." Silver thought the conversation was over, but it wasn't. Pam took a deep breath, then said with surprising briskness, "If you can forgive me and not hate me, then I know Jesus can, too. And I want to ask him to come into my heart."

So right there on the ferry, with the engines rumbling and gulls shrieking, with a surprise spray of water slapping their faces, they clung to the railing and each other and did it.

Silver drove toward Seattle tired, both sorry and glad the week was over. She had a real sense of satisfaction with this final change in Pam, plus the reminder it gave her that you never knew which of your actions would be observed by and affect others.

She almost didn't turn off the main interstate to the other highway to see if the billboard had been changed. What she really wanted was to get home, soak for hours in a tub, and then spend the night in the luxury of a real bed. But at the last minute she decided she should look at the billboard so that she could notify others who had written protests that the letter campaign had been successful.

She slowed as she approached the corner where the billboard was located. Then she pulled onto the shoulder and slammed on the brakes in astonishment. The sign was indeed different now, no curvaceous woman, no picture at all, just words—enormous, startling words, in dramatic black for all the world to see:

Dear Silver,
I was wrong. I made a mistake. I'm sorry. I love you.
Will you marry me?
Chris

Silver just kept staring at the billboard, reading the words over and over. A conflicting array of emotions churned through her. A certain appalled, horrified embarrassment. Other motorists were slowing to look at the billboard, sometimes pointing and laughing. Indignation joined the embarrassment. What was Chris doing, spreading their private problems out for everyone to see? But at the same time she felt an astonished pleasure that he would put his heart on the line with an admission of both love and mistake.

She drove on home, even the longed-for soak in the tub forgotten. The words on the billboard were not memorably poetic. They wouldn't go down in history as the love song of the century or as models of soaring sensitivity. But they sounded honestly heartfelt.

When had he done this? What, exactly, did he feel he was wrong about? Putting his big business deal ahead of Christian commitment? Refusing to acknowledge any need of forgiveness toward Ben? Or maybe this was simply some grandstand play to dazzle her as he'd dazzled the kids at camp with his grand helicopter entrance.

At her apartment, she stared at the open phone book for a solid minute before acting, finally deciding that common courtesy required she at least check on his condition. The search took six phone calls before she located the hospital where he was registered as a patient in room 307.

She smelled of campfire smoke, her shoes still had smudges of mud, and her jeans bore a rip in the knee, courtesy of a last-minute assault by that metal rod in the tent. But she went without bothering to clean up or change clothes, a sudden fear that he could be in a coma or battling death sending her into a near panic.

The door to room 307 was closed. She knocked.

"Come in."

She felt a moment of perverse annoyance when she opened the door. She didn't want him unconscious or on some dramatic life-support system, of course; relief that he wasn't flooded through her. But she also hadn't expected to find him sitting up in bed with what was obviously a big pile of office paperwork scattered around his thigh-to-ankle cast. *Every inch the Mighty Motel Mogul,* she thought a bit crossly.

"Mrs. Oliver was here earlier today." His vague gesture over the papers indicated the secretary had brought them. Not, Silver guessed, on her own initiative. Chris had undoubtedly demanded them.

"How are you?" she asked.

"Broken leg, strained back, bumps and bruises. No big deal."

He also had a black eye, technically a purple-and-green eye, although the lump on his cheekbone was gone. A small tightening of his jaw when he leaned forward to shove the papers aside suggested that the strained back gave him more pain than he cared to admit.

"How long will you be in here?"

He started to shrug, but the movement made him wince. "A few days."

"I saw the billboard," she said in a carefully offhand voice.

"What did you think?"

"It…wasn't what I expected."

"Do I get a critique on the tone and wording and a dressing-down on the fact that I didn't do it in my own handwriting, as I have on certain other of my correspondence?"

Silver ignored his question, countering with one of her own. "What exactly was the apology for?"

"For trying to leap over the Lord's roadblock. For putting my ambitions for worldly success, along with proving something to Ben, ahead of my Christian commitment and doing what the Lord would have me do."

"Isn't it convenient that you hammered the Golden Lighthouse deal through before this revelation occurred to you?"

"What makes you think that?"

"You agreed with me when I suggested at camp that congratulations were in order. You said the deal didn't fall through again. And you didn't arrive in camp until Tuesday."

"Not for lack of trying! That helicopter pilot and I spent the better part of Sunday, Monday, and Tuesday morning just trying to find the island under all that cloud cover. It was like flying through murky vegetable soup looking for one minuscule chunk of carrot."

Silver blinked. "I don't understand."

"I started thinking about everything you said. Not *liking* it, you understand. And throwing up all kinds of arguments about how wrong you were, how forgiveness had nothing to do with Ben and me. And then I postponed my Saturday morning meeting with the Golden Lighthouse lawyers and went to see Ben instead."

"Why?"

"Not some big, mind-opening revelation from God," he

admitted. "But sometimes we get these...spiritual shoves." He paused, then, sounding a little disgruntled to have been treated with such godly forcefulness, added, "To put it more bluntly, like a good kick in the behind."

Silver covered a smile. "I've had those," she agreed. "Was Ben his usual cheery self?"

Chris smiled ruefully. "Yeah. More or less. We small-talked about this and that. Well, *I* small-talked," he corrected, "and Ben sat there looking like he'd swallowed a lemon. Then he turned and looked at me, and I realized that maybe it wasn't so much a sour attitude as a scared bewilderment about who I was. Then he kind of blinked, and recognition came into his eyes, and it suddenly got through to me that he could just...fade away someday. And though my animosity might not bother or matter to him, I'd be stuck with it, just like you said. On an endless treadmill trying to prove something to somebody who was...gone. And I suddenly just started pouring out all the resentment I'd felt toward him over the years."

"Forgiving him?"

He shook his head. "No. Just letting it all out. But after I got it out, he kind of blinked and said, very grudgingly, that maybe he had been a little unfair. We didn't have some emotional, falling-in-each-other's-arms scene, but I said that was okay, I understood. And the forgiveness was there. It just...flooded into my heart. I don't hold anything against him anymore."

"So then you went back and, with conscience freed, happily rammed the Golden Lighthouse deal through."

He grabbed a handful of papers and tossed them in the air in exasperation. "Sil, will you for once in your life *not*—like Superman clearing tall buildings in a single leap—jump to conclusions?"

He didn't give her time to respond to that before he went on.

"Yes, I did feel 'freed.' Freed not to have to prove anything to Ben. I suppose I'm always going to be something of a workaholic, but I've got my priorities straight now."

"Which means—?"

"Which means I got hold of the Golden Lighthouse people and told them I was still interested in the deal, but I had prior commitments for the next two weeks. If at the end of that time the deal was still open, I'd be interested in negotiating with them. If not…" He shrugged lightly.

Silver sorted it out in her head. The deal hadn't gone through, but neither had it collapsed again. Congratulations were in order, not for a successful deal, but because he'd gotten his priorities straight. And she had indeed jumped this tall building in a single leap to wrong conclusions. "I guess I owe you an apology," she admitted.

"You do," he agreed.

"Okay, I apologize."

"I love you, you know."

Silver crossed her arms. "So how come you sound so grumpy about it?"

"I'd expected to be a bridegroom by tomorrow, on my way to a honeymoon backpacking in Costa Rica with my new bride. Instead, here I am trapped in a hospital bed, my lovesick emotions spread all over a highway billboard."

"Oh, Chris," she breathed. "I love you, too." Then she smiled. "Although I haven't yet rented a billboard to announce it."

"So how come you're looking at me as if I just won the Weirdo of the Year Award?" he demanded.

"Proposing via billboard is a rather weird thing to do."

He forgot his strained back, shrugged, and winced again.

"But I…rather like it," she admitted. "Did you notify your

pastor that the wedding scheduled for tomorrow has been called off?"

"Not yet."

"Why not? You're not exactly in shape to stride down the aisle. Although we do still have a perfectly good wedding license."

They looked at each other warily across the expanse of the hospital bed, office papers and love and past arguments spread between them.

"Are you thinking what I'm thinking?" he asked finally.

"Maybe." Then she shook her head. "No, we couldn't do it. It's a crazy idea, totally impossible."

"With love and the Lord, *anything's* possible!"

And so it was that on the following afternoon, one canceled wedding was joyfully uncanceled.

The participants who gathered in the cramped hospital room were few. Colleen stood beside Silver on one side of the bed, smiling even as she occasionally rolled her eyes and muttered, "This is no way to run a wedding." Chris half-sat, half-lay in the bed, a dash of yellow now added to his green-and-purple eye. The best man stood on the other side of the bed. The pastor held his Bible at the foot of the bed. Old Ben, whom Chris had gruffly said at the last minute might like to come, stood off to one side. A nurse stood at the head of the bed, holding the phone with an open line to Idaho so Silver's parents could hear everything.

Both Silver and Chris leaned toward it, their heads only inches apart, as they answered the minister's questions with the words of lifelong promise.

"I do."

"I do."

And then not even a strained back, a broken leg, and a hospital bed could stop the sweet seal of the wedding kiss.

Dear Reader,

This is my third book for Palisades (plus a novella in the Christmas anthology *Mistletoe*), and I hope you've enjoyed reading them as much as I've enjoyed writing them.

My first two Palisades books were set in the time of the Great Depression, so *Dear Silver* is my first one with a contemporary setting. The outward circumstances and problems of that earlier time may be different than they are today, but basic problems of the heart and spirit remain much the same whatever the era. But in any time, with any problem, we can always find our shelter and support in the Lord.

I've especially appreciated you readers who have taken time to write me. Hearing that someone has enjoyed and been uplifted by something you have written, that a reader has found a truth of some special value in the story, is one of the author's greatest joys.

Thanks to all my readers,

Lorena McCourtney

PALISADES...PURE ROMANCE

Diamonds, Shari MacDonald
Stardust, Shari MacDonald
Westward, Amanda MacLean
Stonehaven, Amanda MacLean
Everlasting, Amanda MacLean
Promise Me the Dawn, Amanda MacLean (Premier)
Kingdom Come, Amanda MacLean
Betrayed, Lorena McCourtney
Escape, Lorena McCourtney
Dear Silver, Lorena McCourtney
Voyage, Elaine Schulte

ANTHOLOGIES

A Christmas Joy, Darty, Gillenwater, MacLean
Mistletoe, Ball, Hicks, McCourtney
A Mother's Love, Bergren, Colson, MacLean